STANDING IN THE SUNSHINE

To Alice, Daniel, Mari and Simon Loder, my motivation for fighting and my reason for living when I wanted to die. The future belongs to you all now.

✦ STANDING ✦
✦ IN THE ✦
✦ SUNSHINE ✦

The Story of the
Multiple Sclerosis Breakthrough

CARI LODER

C̲

Published by Century in 1996

3 5 7 9 10 8 6 4 2

© 1996 Cari Loder

Century Ltd
Random House, 20 Vauxhall Bridge Road, London SW1V 2SA

Random House Australia (Pty) Limited
20 Alfred Street, Milsons Point, Sydney,
New South Wales 2061, Australia

Random House New Zealand Limited
18 Poland Road, Glenfield
Auckland 10, New Zealand

Random House South Africa (Pty) Limited
PO Box 337, Bergvlei, South Africa

Random House UK Limited Reg. No. 954009

A CIP catalogue record for this book is available from the
British Library

Papers used by Random House UK Ltd are natural, recyclable products made from wood grown in sustainable forests. The manufacturing processes conform to the environmental regulations of the country of origin.

ISBN 0 7126 7639 2

Typeset by Deltatype Ltd, Ellesmere Port, Cheshire
Printed and bound in the United Kingdom by
Mackays of Chatham plc, Chatham, Kent

◆

ACKNOWLEDGEMENTS

◆

My gratitude goes to those who travelled on the journey with me. You know who you are.

Special thanks go to:

My wonderful medical team Raj, JMH, Dean and Sally who supported me through thick and thin. I hope you all know how special you are.

My friends, especially Gareth, Hilary, Colm, Dave, Maureen, Gill, Di, and Charlie who cheered me on when things were going well and shared the misery with me when things were bad. All I can say is you are the best of friends anyone could wish for.

And lastly, to all my 'friends' on the computer Internet, especially Mollusc, who were all so generous with their time and support, I can never thank you enough.

READERS PLEASE NOTE

In this book I have not disclosed what the drugs used in my treatment are for several reasons.

Firstly, until clinical trials have been conducted I can not say for sure that the treatment will be safe for everyone; indeed, I already know that people with certain medical conditions or who are taking other drugs can not safely use the treatment.

Secondly, until the medical profession has been assured, through the outcome of clinical trials, that the treatment is effective, they will be unlikely to agree to prescribe the necessary drugs.

Please do not try to guess what the drugs are. You will never get it right and at best will be disappointed as other combinations *do not work*. At worst you may do yourself harm. The anti-depressant mentioned is *one specific* anti-depressant. The mention of cola is by no means the full story. The B12 is indeed used in the treatment but the exact dose and frequency is essential and has not been disclosed here.

I am sure that many readers will be disappointed at hearing that a solution to MS may well be here but that they can not have it yet. All I can ask is that you bear with me a while longer. Scotia, the pharmaceutical company who have taken an exclusive licence on my patent, will be conducting clinical trials during 1996 and we will ensure that information about the trials gets out as they progress.

I beg you not to try to contact me to find out what the drugs are. There will not be much longer to wait before everyone can know about and have access to the treatment.

Cari P. J. Loder
1995

CONTENTS

PROLOGUE

HAVING MS *is like being on any long journey, but without a map to guide you. You sometimes get lost. You encounter steep hills, deep ravines and stony paths. But there is also beautiful scenery along the way and you meet fellow travellers who often become friends, if only in passing.*

Before I was diagnosed I knew nothing at all about MS. Unusually, perhaps, I had never knowingly met a person with MS in my life. I say unusually because since I was diagnosed every single person I mention it to seems to know at least one other person with MS. Many have family members who have been diagnosed. After I received my diagnosis I became obsessed with finding out about the disease in order to try and understand what was happening to me. What I discovered shocked me. Despite the fact that it had been identified in 1827, little was known about MS. I subsequently discovered that MS is still classified as an "orphan" disease since the known number of sufferers worldwide does not exceed one million. This means the government does not fund research into the disease. Strange, as MS is the most common acquired neurological condition in the world. If the costs to society of disability benefit, supported/ sheltered housing, institutionalisation, supportive therapies, hospitalisation and drug treatments are taken into consideration, then the price of not funding research becomes extremely high. Even on exclusively financial grounds.

What follows is a little of what I have discovered during the course of my research.

Multiple Sclerosis is a medical paradox. The disease was first named in 1827 and has formerly been called Disseminated Sclerosis. Its cause remains an almost complete mystery although currently many theories abound, from a viral cause, to genetics, to environmental factors to a combination of them all.

MS is a progressive disease of the central nervous system (CNS) in which scattered patches of myelin (the protective covering of the nerve fibres) in the brain and spinal cord are destroyed. It is thought to be an auto-immune disorder in which the body's defence system begins to treat the myelin sheath of the nerves in the brain and spine as a foreign substance, an invader, gradually destroying it, with subsequent scarring and sometimes damage to some of the underlying nerve fibres. If you think of the nerves in the brain and spine as electric cables, with the myelin sheath being the equivalent of the plastic coating, then you have a good model to understand MS. If you connect a bulb to an electric socket by a wire, then the electricity gets through to the bulb and it lights up. If, however, part of the plastic coating is stripped off and it is touched by another wire, then the electricity will short-circuit and the bulb will flicker or not light up at all. So it is, roughly, with MS except that the electricity 'leaks' out through the demyelinated areas on the nerve or the current is simply slowed down on its way to the muscles or skin or wherever it was going.

There are approximately 80,000 people diagnosed with MS in the UK and roughly one million worldwide. One of the cruellest things about MS is the fact that it strikes people most often in their twenties and early thirties just as their careers are beginning. However, some people are diagnosed much earlier or later, some in their mid-teens and others even as late as the age of fifty. The age at diagnosis does not always reflect, even marginally, the age at onset as it is extremely difficult for people to get their early symptoms taken seriously by the medical profession. Many people subsequently diagnosed with MS may have had fleeting symptoms for many years before they reached a level of severity that could no longer be ignored. It is the most common acquired disease of the nervous system in young adults. In the relatively high-risk temperate areas the incidence is approximately one in every 1,000 people. The ratio of women to men sufferers is roughly three to one, a fact that has yet to be explained.

A genetic factor seems to be indicated since relatives of affected people are eight times more likely than others to develop the condition. Environment is hypothesised by some to potentially play a part as MS is five times more common in temperate zones (such as Europe and the US) than in the tropics.

In July 1995 it was announced in the national press that a team of Southampton University medical researchers had made a discovery in their search for genetic clues to MS. The team has been examining the genes responsible for producing the myelin membrane. They claim to have already discovered that myelin contains "rho" proteins which act as molecular switches, transmitting signals involved in the formation and movement of membranes in various types of cells.

The severity of MS varies wildly among sufferers. It is characterised by a patchy pattern of disabilities, variable in both site and time, with dramatic unpredictable deterioration or improvement. Someone may be completely normal one day and severely disabled the next, or blind one day and wake up with normal sight the next. This inability to predict what is going to happen next is, for MS sufferers, one of the most difficult psychological things to deal with. You can not plan on the basis of what you might be able to do tomorrow let alone in two years time. This, for me, was one of the hardest things to deal with. In my professional life I was frequently being asked if I could give a presentation at a conference anything up to seven months down the line. I was faced with the choice of either saying yes and, more likely than not, having to let the organisers down at the last minute, or simply saying that I couldn't commit to being able to do it.

MS usually starts in early adult life. It may be active for a brief period of time and then resume years later, or it may be progressive from the outset. The symptoms of MS read like a horror story and they vary according to which parts of the brain and spinal cord are affected. Spinal cord damage can cause tingling, numbness or a feeling of constriction in any part of the body (the infamous "MS hug"). The feet and hands may feel heavy and become weak. Spasticity (increased muscle rigidity) and paralysis sometimes develop. The nerves to the bladder and/or bowel may be involved, causing either retention or incontinence. Damage to the myelin in the brain may lead to fatigue, vertigo, numbness, weakness or pain in the face (trigeminal neuralgia).

Symptoms may occur one at a time in isolation or in combination and may last from minutes to years. In some sufferers, relapses may be brought on by injury, infection or physical or emotional stress. I fully believe that MS is made worse by stress. In the eighteen months leading up to the onset of my MS I had been working like a lunatic, regularly being at the office seven days a week from six in the morning to eleven at night. I knew that something was going to break in the end, but was expecting it to be nervous exhaustion, not MS. Many MS sufferers can tell of car accidents or serious viral illnesses prior to the MS showing itself. All MS sufferers will say that periods of physical or emotional stress makes their MS symptoms worse or can, in some cases, precipitate a relapse.

The severity of attacks varies considerably from one person to another. In some people the disease can be essentially benign with only mild relapses and long symptom-free periods throughout life, with very few permanent effects. In others a series of flare-ups leave some disability, but then there is no further deterioration. Some sufferers become gradually more disabled from the first attack and are bedridden and incontinent in early middle life or younger. A few people suffer severe disability within the first few years of the disease.

There are different ways in which MS shows itself. The most common is a form known as Remitting-Relapsing (RR). This is where the person may have an initial attack which resolves after a few weeks and then may be attack and symptom free (in remission) for weeks, months or years before another attack hits. After a period of perhaps fifteen to twenty years the remissions may finally stop occurring and the person will often become progressively more disabled. This stage is known as Secondary Chronic Progressive (SCP). The other form, Primary Chronic Progressive (PCP), is where the person has no remissions from the start and simply deteriorates from the outset.

A person affected by MS may have additional problems, such as painful muscle spasms, urinary tract infections, constipation, skin ulceration, changes of mood between euphoria and depression, or problems with short-term memory or speech. In other words, MS can affect virtually every part of a sufferer's life.

There is no single diagnostic test for MS. Confirmation of the disease is usually done by the exclusion of all other possible conditions such as meningitis, sarcoidosis, lupus, a stroke or a tumour. A neurologist may often perform tests to help confirm the diagnosis, including a lumbar puncture (removal of a sample of fluid from the spine for laboratory analysis) to look for the evidence of myelin debris, evoked potential responses (tracing electrical activity in the brain) and Magnetic Resonance Imaging (MRI) scans to look for patches of inflammation or scarring.

The search for a complete cure is still in progress. Many patients claim to have benefited from making changes to their diet, including the addition of sunflower or evening primrose oils. Hyperbaric Oxygen (HBO) treatment was widely acclaimed as a treatment in the mid-1970s and some groups of patients financed the building of treatment facilities in the UK. Previously, however, no treatment has been found to be of more than slight benefit for large numbers of patients. The most widely used treatment are Corticosteroids which are regularly prescribed to alleviate the symptoms of an acute attack.

HBO has been used for several years for the treatment of MS for large numbers of people in the States, Italy and the Soviet

Union as well as in the UK. Although patients with chronic progressive MS reported some improvement after a course of HBO lasting several weeks, they reverted to their previous level once the treatment stopped. When the treatment was examined under double-blind conditions, the unanimous outcome was that HBO had no effect on any objective measure of the disease with the exception of slight improvement in bladder control in some people. There is a concern about this treatment inasmuch as exposure to oxygen at levels that are too high for too long periods could result in serious side-effects such as blindness or convulsions. It was observed in trials that these side effects can happen to some people even when treated correctly. The medical profession's opinion seems to be that HBO has no therapeutic value whatsoever for MS, that it is very expensive and that its use carries significant risk to the patient.

Despite many false-hope treatments, there has never been an effective treatment for MS, other than a few drugs that provide some symptomatic relief, such as Baclofen for spasticity and Oxybutanin for bladder incontinence.

The history of MS is punctuated with false-dawn cures, including, most recently, snake venom therapy and bee sting therapy. Bovine myelin (cow brain) ingestion has also been thought to "distract" the body's autoimmune system away from attacking the human myelin. Desperate people will, inevitably, clutch at desperate measures in the face of the medical profession's inability to offer any hope. MS sufferers have tried the gluten-free diet, high doses of evening primrose oil or fish oils, the "saturated fat-free" diet, and taking doses of megavitamins. People have experimented with aromatherapy, acupuncture, hypnosis, yoga and spiritual healing. My personal attitude is that, if it is not ridiculously expensive and is not harmful, then sufferers should do whatever they feel helps. There is little doubt that doing *anything* that enables you to feel less than totally impotent in the face of this evil disease must, by definition, be beneficial in some form or other, if only psychologically.

The rationales for many of the unorthodox treatments are exemplified by that of snake venom therapy. The snake venom used is a combination of cobra, krait and water moccasin venoms which is injected under the skin. The idea of using snake venom in MS treatment came about as a result of a person who worked with snakes being bitten by one of them. He subsequently developed a range of neurological symptoms, some of which suggested that his nervous system was being adversely affected. The use of snake venom therapy has not been investigated scientifically. It has been suggested as a treatment for arthritis, lupus, herpes simplex, herpes zoster, muscular dystrophy, Parkinson's disease, myasthenia gravis and amyotrophic lateral sclerosis, as well as for MS.

Probably the most highly publicised medically *bona fide* treatment for MS to date is Beta Interferon. Beta Interferon 1-b is made by Schering and marketed in the States under the name Betaseron by Berlex and in the UK as Betaferon. Beta Interferon 1-a, known also as Rebif, is made by Ares Serono. Another type of Beta Interferon 1-a is made by Biogen. The evidence to date from American and Canadian trials suggests that it may be possible to delay (not abolish) the progress of the disease in newly diagnosed and mild remitting/relapsing forms of MS. Long-term effects of the drug are unknown but side effects (of which 65 are listed by Berlex in the *Physicians' Desk Reference*) include injection site reactions (red blotches where the needle goes in), nausea, chills and a flu-like reaction. Exactly how it works is not known, although the drug has a role in regulating the immune system, and appears to slow down the excessive activity of immune system cells (T-cells and monocytes) implicated in the attack of the protective myelin sheath surrounding the nerves.

Corticosteroids, Corticotropin, Azathioprine, Cyclophosphamide and Beta Interferon have all had a substantial effect on the care of MS patients inasmuch as doctors at least have something to inject us with or make us swallow. Whether we actually choose to swallow the promotional hype is quite another matter. Some mild symptomatic benefit may be experienced by some people. The use of MRI scanning and more sensitive clinical outcome measures will possibly enable the medical researchers to complete clinical trials in a fraction of the time required for earlier trials. However, there is a risk that although it may be possible to design and use measures of objective quantification for the researcher, they fail to produce significant change in the patient.

In the light of their inability to do anything to prevent the relentless but unpredictable progress of the disease, MS seems to be a diagnosis that doctors particularly dread because it renders them so helpless. It must be very hard for someone who entered their profession in order to heal people to have little choice but to stand back and watch the disintegration of full, active lives. The doctors must often feel like bystanders at a wake.

The diagnosis of many neurological diseases is a difficult and often time-consuming affair. Even when the doctor has arrived at a diagnosis of MS the patient is often not told that they have the disease. In some instances patients are sent away with the cause of their symptoms unexplained and are left to deal with them as best they can. To the layman it seems strange for the medical profession to tell what sounds like lies or, to use the official jargon, non-disclosure of the diagnosis which used to be, and to some extent still is, a very widespread practice. Doctors often legitimise this practice by saying that even if they are clear that their patient has MS it is possible that the symptoms may disappear due to there being a spontaneous remission and the person may remain that way for some considerable time. Some doctors seem to think that it would be better if the person concerned should not know they have MS and, therefore, worry about the long-term consequences. A form of "If you do not know that the sword of Damocles is hanging over your head then it will not bother you". They justify this by observing that stress can precipitate another MS attack and the diagnosis in itself can be stressful. The problem is, of course, whether you know it is there or not does not alter the fact that it is indeed hanging over you. And maybe if you know it is there you can take certain measures to move out of its way, such as resting more, eating healthily and generally taking care of yourself.

◆

CHAPTER ONE

BUILDING BLOCKS

◆

I WAS born in Blackheath, south-east London in January 1961, the youngest child of three and christened Caroline Penelope Jane. My sister Viki is the oldest being three years older than me and my brother, Clive, is sixteen months younger than her. My father was a civil servant at the Civil Aviation Authority and my mother spent her time bringing up the three of us until we were all at secondary school when she became a secretary at a local school. We lived in a normal two-storey house where my sister and I shared a bedroom. We had a reasonable sized back garden with a pond where I spent many happy hours as a young child playing with the newts. Black-heath, so called because it was the scene of many burials as a result of the Black Death, was very middle class and, as far as I was concerned, boring.

I was introduced to the world of doctors at a very early age as I was born with a squint which had to be operated on at the age of five in order to correct it. After the operation I wore an eye patch for some time to try to strengthen the weak eye. I used to think wearing a patch was really neat as I could get away with only closing one eye in prayers at school assembly. This was followed by eleven years of wearing glasses and having to attend appointments at the Royal Eye Hospital. I was also born with a congenitally small jaw which meant that from an early age I had to have teeth taken out at regular intervals in order to make room for the next ones to come through. I got used to being prodded and poked, checked and questioned by doctors right from the start.

At the age of ten I developed a rather nasty lung condition which resulted in my being off school for quite some time. The disease showed itself as fluid on the lung which meant I was very short of breath. My favourite trick was to breathe out as far as I could so that people could hear the fluid in my lung bubbling! I was also running a very high temperature much of the time. The disease refused to respond to a whole range of medicines and treatments and so I was finally put on steroids which, thankfully, eventually did the trick. Little did I know then that this would teach me lessons that would be quite useful when dealing with developing MS.

I remember one particular appointment at the chest clinic where the doctor wanted to take a blood test. I was scared to death of needles and also partly delirious due to the high temperature I was running. The doctor appeared pissed off with me for not cooperating. I was crying and yelling and thrashing around as he tried to put the tourniquet on and put the needle in my arm. He finally got someone to physically hold me down so he could take the blood. The doctor's name was Vardik, a gaunt and angular man, whom I promptly dubbed vampire Vardik. Actually the name suited him down to the ground.

I think that having had to deal with the sight, teeth and lung problems I grew up somewhat faster than normal, as many children facing illnesses do. I believe that dealing with personal adversity as a child made me a lot stronger and more autonomous than would otherwise have been the case. For as long as I can remember, the concept of authority was something I was simply unable to understand. I suppose that when you are a child and are ill and grown-ups can not make things better, you cease to rely on them or trust them and, therefore, rely only on yourself. I certainly never believed that adults were any better or more able than me.

I grew up as insatiably curious and irreverent as Kipling's Elephant's Child who asked so many questions that he was always getting into trouble. Quite uncomfortably and certainly unwittingly, I developed what may well have been the perfect psychological profile for pioneer research. Whenever I encountered something that I did not understand but which interested me, I wanted to know how it worked and why, and, just like the Elephant's Child, quite often my curiosity got me into trouble. I remember that, from an early age, inventing toys for myself simply through observing things and playing with the idea. For instance, I developed a range of toys using pipe-cleaners bent into a hook with a piece of cotton attached and a weight at the bottom, which meant they could balance on a tiny wire point at any angle without falling over. I am not aware of anyone having taught me how to do that. It was simply a case of observation, trial and error and having an insatiably curious mind.

From the time I could read I was obsessed with books. I was a voracious reader of pretty much anything I could get my hands on. I was particularly enthralled by science fiction and loved the idea that new things could be developed which sorted out problems that existed in the real world. I also found it fascinating that many of the science fiction ideas were simply a case of starting from a known quantity and developing it further into the realms of fantasy and supposition. I used to love day-dreaming about how to develop new objects or mechanisms to solve currently insoluble problems. My favourite series of books at that time was the *Dune Trilogy* by Frank Herbert.

I was so obsessed with reading that I always read the back of the cereal package at breakfast. I know that when I was in my early teens I worked out that I was allergic to a certain colouring used in food (Tartrazine) simply by observing my reaction to certain foods and drinks and identifying the only common ingredient in all of them. This was long before I was aware that many children do indeed react badly to Tartrazine, which was subsequently withdrawn from usage. This habit of reading ingredient lists was one which I never lost and which, in due course, was going to be significant in making the breakthrough on the MS treatment. I wonder just how many people habitually read the list of ingredients on the back of cola cans?

When I went to secondary school, Prendergast Grammar School, in Catford I was, for the first time, exposed to science. I was one of the first cohort of schoolchildren to take part in the Schools Council Integrated Science Project (SCISP) which meant that we were taught biology, chemistry and physics as a single subject up to and including O levels. I took to this approach like a duck to water. SCISP differed from single-subject science teaching inasmuch as we were required to design our own experiments to research certain phenomena, observe the results and write up the outcomes. Looking back on it I realise just how well this prepared me for making the breakthrough with the MS treatment. It essentially laid the groundwork for me to undertake pioneering empirical research.

I achieved straight A grades in my O level science examinations and went on to study biology and chemistry at A level. Unfortunately, as the old single-subject A level curriculum was unchanged we had, therefore, not covered it in enough depth due to studying SCISP at O level and I did not do at all well in the examinations. I achieved two unremarkable grades in my science A levels which were not good enough to enable me to go on and study science at university. I had actually set my heart on studying to be a chemical engineer and my chemistry teacher, Roy, reckoned I had the natural affinity with chemistry to be able to do it. I remember him saying to me, on several occasions, that one of my biggest personal problems was that I never believed what anyone told me was fact until I had checked it out for myself but that, as far as science went, it was my biggest strength. So, paradoxically, it was this inability to trust anyone that turned me into an empirical researcher.

I used to love working in the school science laboratory when I was studying for my A Levels. I was in my element surrounded by test tubes, bunsen burners and chemicals. I loved the peace and quiet of the lab and the smell of the chemicals. I also liked the element of danger in working with quite nasty chemicals in organic chemistry. Strangely enough, it was in the lab at school that I inadvertently discovered an effective treatment for migraines which I had suffered from badly since the age of eleven. I had a bad migraine one day and was working on an experiment when I sniffed the test tube I had just put one of the chemicals in and noticed that the pain in my head went away almost instantly! I tried this on a couple of occasions when I had a migraine and finally told Roy about it. He asked me what the chemical was and I told him that it was 1.1.1-Trichloroethane, a solvent. He grinned at me and said that it would indeed help my migraines as it would act as a vaso-dilator (or constrictor, I can't remember which now). I very naughtily got hold of a little bottle of the chemical to carry around with me in case I got a migraine! I subsequently discovered, again as a result of my habit of reading labels, that the chemical was the solvent in Tippex thinner fluid. So I had easy access to my magic migraine treatment.

Roy was very special to me during my school years. He was probably in his early forties and was still full of enthusiasm for teaching science. He was quite unlike the other teachers inasmuch as he laughed and joked with the pupils and talked to us about his family and his life outside school. He also had an infectious smile that inspired trust. He treated me almost as a friend instead of the way most teachers treat children. He really seemed to care about me and like me. When, from time to time, I was not performing terribly well in class he would not give me a hard time but would take me to one side and ask me what was wrong. Because my home life was a little unsettled during my later school years, I really needed an adult who would look out for me and who I could talk to. Roy filled that gap and gave me something no other person had been able to. He gave me self-confidence. He communicated to me that he believed in me and, as I trusted him, I began to believe in myself for the first time.

My other great passion at that time was art. I would spend hours every evening at home working on intricate black ink graphic pictures. Once again it was the peace and quiet of total concentration that I found addictive. I would get so absorbed in the work that I was unaware of time passing or of anything going on around me. I became very insular, and almost introverted and resented time taken away from being able to work on my art. Again I had found something else that I naturally excelled at. My art work was the only thing I did not need anyone else to tell me was good. What other people thought of my art work was irrelevant to me. I knew it was good and that was enough for me. This was a first for me, up to that point I had been constantly looking for external validation of anything I did which, more often than not, I never got.

As I had not managed to get the A Levels I needed to pursue science at university and, in order to gain a further A level equivalent, I managed to secure a place at Goldsmiths College to take a foundation course in art and design where I specialised in graphic design. I didn't really gain much from that year at college as all the other students were doing really 'arty' things like pottery or oil painting. I had no affinity whatsoever for other artistic mediums and so simply stuck to my graphic work which was not deemed by the tutors to be the 'real' thing.

At the end of the course I started to apply to polytechnics and universities to take a degree in art. Unfortunately I was not offered a place and therefore had to, once again, reassess my future career.

Every summer for the previous four years I had helped run a children's summer holiday club for the local church. My ability with art and the fact that I played the guitar meant that I could offer quite a lot to the holiday club. I worked with one of the other organisers, David, to plan the theme of the club each year and to prepare the art work for the backdrop and the quiz boards. I thoroughly enjoyed every minute of the planning and preparation as well as actually helping to run the club for a week each summer. This was the first experience I had of being part of a team and I discovered that it really was good fun. We had about one hundred children between the ages of three and fifteen at the club each day. That was the first time I had worked with children and I discovered that I loved being with them and, much to my amazement, they liked me as well. David was a school teacher at that time and consequently I was working alongside a professional. I began to ponder the idea of being a teacher.

When my plans for pursuing first science and then art fell through, I decided to combine my fondness of children with my passion for art and applied for a place on a teacher-training degree course at Teesside Polytechnic. Three weeks before the new academic year was due to start I was called up to Teesside for an interview. I really did not think I stood a hope in hell of securing a place on the course but tried my best at the interview. After the group and individual interviews had been conducted, the course tutor, Fred Machin, came out to find me in the corridor where I was awaiting the outcome. He stood there smiling and said, "Well, I am very pleased to be able to offer you a place on the course." I think my expression must have been completely inappropriate to the news he had just imparted (I was totally convinced he was going to say I hadn't got a place) as he reached out, took my hand and, looking me straight in the eye, said "Did you hear what I said? It's OK. You've got a place." I guess I should have realised there and then that Teesside was going to be a rather special place.

It was something of a culture shock to move from middle-class, sanitised Blackheath to the rough and ready world of the north-east of England. I also had not had much time at all to adjust to the idea of moving "up north" or studying teaching. The first day of the degree course we were asked to introduce ourselves to each other in the introductory sessions. In the first session I made a snap decision to change my name, and therefore my identity, to Cari. I felt that it was time to leave my less than successful and not totally happy past behind me and reinvent myself.

Perhaps because of the somewhat chaotic way I ended up at Teesside I was less than committed to what I was doing and consequently my first year was marked by undone essays and non-attendance at teaching practice. At the end of my first year I was in imminent danger of being thrown off the course. However, the staff on my course at Teesside Poly *were* rather special. Instead of just leaving me to fail, they set up a series of interviews with me in the space of a day. As I ran the gamut of tutor after tutor asking me why I was not turning up to lectures and not completing my course work, I moved from a position of indifference to one of stark fear of failure. The second to last interview was with my psychology lecturer Mike who, although I did not know it at the time, was about to become my salvation. Mike was a down-to-earth genius in psychology from Birmingham who, from the time we got to know each other, referred to me as "kiddo". He had the most gorgeous dark brown eyes which communicated both warmth and wicked humour.

By then I was fully expecting another ear-bashing about not doing work or falling asleep in his lectures. However, he completely disarmed me by chatting to me about his hobby of making silver jewellery. After a while he looked at me and asked in a rather offhand manner, "Is there any particular reason why you are mucking around on the course, Cari?" It was the first time I had been confronted with that question and I found myself at a loss to justify my behaviour, so I shrugged and told him that there really wasn't a reason. He nodded and said "OK, see you next year then."

I left his office feeling rather emotionally off-balance, no longer knowing what I actually wanted to do, leave Teesside or make a go of the degree. My last interview was with Neil, the director of the teacher-training college, a man I had never had cause to speak to before. I knocked on his office door, fully expecting to be thrown off the course by him. I went in to find him sitting in his directorial chair with his feet up on his desk. He asked me to take a seat, threw a cigarette across the room at me, and said, "OK Cari, you've fucked up your first year, do you still want to stay on the course?" I was completely taken aback. I thought for all of two seconds and said, "Yes, I want to stay", and that was the end of the matter. He grinned at me and said, "OK, we knew you would actually. You see we have known all along that you can do it, the only problem is that you don't seem to have realised it yet." Here again was another example of what Roy, my chemistry teacher, had done for me. These people believed in me for some unknown reason. I responded as I had with Roy. If they believed in me then I *must* be able to do it!

During the next two years the staff, particularly Mike, ensured that I had all the practical and emotional support I needed to build my self-confidence, something I had always been severely lacking in. As a consequence I began to achieve in my studies. I discovered that I really enjoyed studying and teaching. I started to choose to work with remedial secondary schoolchildren on my teaching practice. Actually the reason I chose to work with them was that one of the subjects I was teaching was maths, and my maths was appallingly bad! I reckoned that I could at least teach remedial maths without being out of my league. It was Mike who pointed out to me later that the other reason I wanted to work with these children was that the system had failed them and therefore, if I failed in teaching them, it was not necessarily a reflection on my ability. He was right, of course. It was my fear of failure that constantly drove me.

It was during this time that I became a workaholic for the first time. I would get up at half past five in the morning and get the bus up to the college with the steel workers. I loved starting the day with no one else around. Once again it was the peace and quiet and isolation that I liked so much. The college was up in the Eston Hills and I remember the feeling of total calm as I arrived before it was fully light in the morning and could watch the mist slowly clear from the hills as the sun came up. When I was not in lectures or out on teaching practice I would spend all of my time in the canteen writing essays, working on my art, or analysing data from the research for my dissertation. The other students knew to leave me alone when I was working there. I got so absorbed in what I was doing that, much of the time, I was oblivious to what was going on around me. So I was more often than not on my own. As a result the staff would often stop by and have a cup of coffee with me. Many of my conversations with Mike took place there. He would discuss articles he had read, or debate points of analysis with me. It was due to this that my knowledge broadened well beyond what I was being taught on the course. Mike and the other staff made me feel as if I was almost one of them.

At the end of my three years at Teesside I was having a drink with Mike and Neil in the college bar and mentioned to them how important the events at the end of my disastrous first year had been. They both chuckled and told me that the whole day had been carefully stage-managed in advance. I am still amazed that they had been sufficiently concerned about me to take the time to work out how to give me an effective psychological kick up the backside, and then to make sure that for the following two years I was consistently supported and encouraged.

During those years I became fascinated by psychology and wrote a dissertation on the psychological profiles of schoolchildren in receipt of remedial education called "Personality, Self-Concept and Academic Achievement". I found that, like me, they shared poor self-worth and expectations. I discovered for the first time that achievement is addictive.

When I had completed my teacher training degree I was, obviously, hoping to get a teaching post. However, there were not many jobs around in Teesside at that time so, once again, I started to reassess my future career. I decided to try and get a place on a Master's degree course to become an educational psychologist. I applied for a place on a course at Lancaster University and was immediately accepted, as long as I passed my first degree, although securing funding for the place was a problem.

At the end of my first degree I was convinced that I must have failed my final exams. The staff knew that I had applied for a place at Lancaster University and they were also aware that I was very despondent about my exams. I was on the verge of giving up the idea of pursuing the Master's degree. One day, some weeks before the degree results were due to be given out, Neil called me into his office, sat me down, and said, "Cari we can't cope with this any longer. You cannot give up your future academic career now. You have passed your degree. OK?" I can not remember exactly how I responded to the news but I am pretty sure that he had to tell me a couple of times before it sank in! Looking back on that day it was incredibly kind of the course team to, once again, realise how I was feeling and do something about it. I fully believe that if I had gone to any other higher education institution I would never have developed the way I did at Teesside and probably would have failed the degree. Maybe some things are just meant to be.

In due course I managed to get a scholarship from the governors of my secondary school which, with financial support from my parents and doing part-time work at the university, allowed me to pursue the Master's degree.

It was at the end of the Master's course, in the July of 1984, that I now can say almost certainly that the MS began. I had been working exceptionally hard for the whole year and was, therefore, under quite a lot of stress. I began to notice that bits of me were going numb, but only little things like the odd toe, so I never paid it any attention. It is only with hindsight that I now recognise the signs.

By now I was completely hooked on doing academic research and so decided to try and study for a PhD at Lancaster. Shortly after beginning I was asked to do a piece of consultancy research work for the Commonwealth Secretariat in London, which I happily agreed to as I needed the money. Not long after successfully completing that piece of work the Commonwealth Secretariat offered me a six month job in London. So I relocated to central London and started my first real employment as a research assistant working on an International Student Mobility conference. However, as the end of my contract drew near I was approached by another agency, the Overseas Students Trust, who needed a research assistant for a short time to assist by inputting data on a computer. I duly undertook the work and so became familiar with computers and spreadsheets for the first time. When I had completed that term of employment I found myself with no source of income and, almost by mistake, found myself providing a freelance bibliographic research and computer training service to academics and people who were buying Amstrad PCW computers from an electronics shop on Bond Street.

And so my weird and wonderful career continued for several months until a research officer at the Institute of Education heard about me, from a colleague who I had provided training for on her Amstrad PCW, and approached me to help her out for three weeks on a research project. I was happy to do so as I, once again, needed the money. Shortly after I started working at the Institute of Education the research officer contracted a severe form of meningitis and consequently was likely to be away from work for a long time. I was asked to step in and take over her full-time job until such time as she returned to work. And so my career as an academic researcher began in earnest. As a result I have now been working at the Institute of Education for ten years, firstly as a research assistant and then as a research officer and, from 1993, as a lecturer. It still amazes me that the Institute appointed me as a lecturer against national competition when I was a poor bet, to say the least, as by then the MS had taken hold. In a strange way I think I did better in the interview due to the fact that I didn't believe that anyone in their right mind would appoint me. Consequently I didn't feel as if I had anything to lose and was very relaxed about the whole thing.

During those years I began to give presentations about my research at conferences and obviously had to write research reports and, in due course, books. The thing I always enjoyed most about my job as an academic though was the empirical research. I always liken doing research to being like a child on Christmas morning. The planning and execution of the research project was like the pre-Christmas preparations with all the build-up of excitement that goes with it. When I had the data collected and analysed it was like unwrapping the presents. You had no idea what you were going to find and it might turn out to be something amazing. I still get a buzz out of it even now. I also learned to love speaking about the research at conferences. The first time I had to do it, back in 1985, I was nearly sick with fear and stumbled over words and blushed furiously. I can't remember quite how I moved from that position of stark fear to actually enjoying public speaking but I reached a point where I loved doing it. It came as something of a revelation to me that people actually wanted to hear what I had to say!

I should really not be too surprised at my recent move into biochemical and neurological research given my past record! Looking back on my life I can see how nearly everything I have done has, in some way, contributed to enabling me to be in a position to have made the discovery about the MS treatment. I think one of the biggest lessons I have learned is that no experience is wasted even though it may seem so at the time.

If it had not been for studying science at school, I would not have had the foundation in chemistry to work out the biochemical interactions of my treatment. If I had not become so obsessed with psychology I would not have been able to offer emotional support to the people on my trial to the extent that I have. If it were not for my interest in computers I would not have found my way onto the computer Internet and so would not have met a food technologist in New Zealand who helped me to work out the dose of the vital ingredient in cola. If it were not for my professional experience in conducting empirical research I would have been unable to conduct trials with myself and others. If it were not for my early exposure to the medical profession I might have been cowed by their authority and, therefore, might not have been able to question their opinions and put to them my own ideas.

As I am writing this in September 1995, I am 34 years old and only one month away from my three-year anniversary of developing MS. I am still single (and have every intention of remaining so) and live in my own studio flat a few minutes' walk from the Institute of Education. Since October 1992 my life has changed beyond all recognition. I can't believe that so much has happened to me in the space of three years. It has all happened so fast. In October 1992 suddenly I had MS, and then twenty-two months later it had gone, and then out of the blue I had worked out why and then, in quick succession, I had filed the patent and had people on my trial and they were getting better. Then a TV documentary was being made about the story and a drug company had taken out an exclusive licence on the patent and I had a contract with a publisher to write this book. I dare not think too hard about my future. I have no idea at all what it holds for me now. Clinical trials for the treatment will be starting in 1996 and, all being well, the treatment ought to be available to everyone by about 1999. Maybe MS will be close to becoming largely a thing of the past by the end of the millennium.

◆

CHAPTER TWO

PATIENT POWER

◆

MY HORROR story begins in October 1992, three months short of my thirty-second birthday. I was a research officer at London University where I am now a lecturer. I had high aspirations for my future career and was working very hard. My aim was to be the youngest female vice-chancellor ever in a UK university. I had just been to a conference in Washington DC in January 1992 and had loved every minute of it. Except for the fact that I kept slipping over in the street, which I simply put down to the icy ground and my new shoes.

If someone had told me prior to the 12th of October 1992 that my life was about to fall apart I would have laughed and told them not to be stupid. But that is exactly what happened. Not immediately you understand. Not the terrible, sudden tragedy of a car crash, but the beginning of tragedy nonetheless. The point beyond which there is no going back. The point you look back on and say "If only I could turn back the clock". The time you will come to view as the end of your former life, the beginning of a waking nightmare that seems to have no end.

I woke up at 7.30 in the morning feeling dizzy and unsteady. This in itself was not all that unusual; it had happened several times in the past ten years and it had always gone away after an hour or so of extra sleep. As usual I put it down to being overly tired and stressed out.

This time the dizziness persisted through the week. Every time I stood up to get something from the other side of my office I felt woozy and a bit sick and had to sit down again fast. It felt just like you do when you are travel sick. When I was walking home from the office and went to cross a road I would look in both directions to check the traffic was clear and would start to walk straight across the road but would stagger in the direction I last looked! After four days I went to see my GP, Dr Wilson, who thought then that it was an inner ear virus leading to loss of balance. He prescribed some travel sickness tablets and sent me on my way. A week later the dizziness was joined by a sharp pain in my right eye. My sight began to deteriorate. I had suffered from migraines since the age of eleven and they had often affected my eyesight (or so I then thought). Now I developed an agonising pain behind my right eye which got worse if I looked upward. Shortly after the pain started I began to notice that everything looked dim, as if I was seeing everything through a fog. I also began to notice other weird effects. I had a tapestry of a peacock on the wall in my flat which had various shades of red in it and I realised one evening that the reds no longer looked right, they were more pastel than anything else. Something that really bugged me was that, if I was walking down the street and there was a scrap of white paper lying on the pavement, it looked to me as if it was glowing. The same effect happened when looking at something typed on white paper. For a start the paper looked grey instead of white and the black letters looked as if they were outlined in a brilliant fluorescent white.

I went back to Dr Wilson again to explain to him what else had gone wrong. He was based in a local community practice which, as it is in central London, had a huge patient list. Many of the people waiting were residents of a local hostel for the homeless so the waiting room was always rather chaotic, noisy and at times dangerous, as many of the people were on drink or drugs and could be very unpredictable. It was probably the last place you wanted to be if you were feeling unwell! I was finally called and went to his office. There were always two or more locums working at this practice and, as a result, no doctor had his own permanent office. The consulting rooms were empty and devoid of any personal effects or the normal clutter. I was not really worried about what was happening to me and still assumed, as I always did, that it was something pretty trivial.

I went in and sat down and he asked me how things had been in the interval since he'd last seen me. I explained about the dizziness getting worse and my sight deteriorating. He looked into my eyes with his ophthalmoscope and made no comment. He then asked me to lie down on my back on the examination couch and told me to lift up my right leg and put my right heel on my left knee and run it down my leg to the ankle and then back up again. I wondered what on earth he was doing but was somewhat surprised when my right foot kept slipping off my left leg. I then had to repeat the process with the other leg, which I couldn't do either. Once again he made no comment. He then asked me to reach out with one hand and touch his hand with a

29

finger and then touch my nose and to do this several times over and then to do the same with the other hand. I kept missing his hand and my nose, which I thought was funny, and got the giggles every time I poked myself in the eye. He asked me to take off my shoes and scratched the soles of my feet with a pointed stick. After that he told me to stand up and walk heel to toe across the room. I had always been able to do that with no trouble at all but this time I wobbled all over the place. I would certainly have failed the drunk test! Once again I got the giggles. Then he told me to stand with my heels together and close my eyes and to try and stand still. I promptly fell backwards and he had to catch me to prevent me from falling over.

When he seemed to be saying that it was probably a problem with my inner ear and sent me away again telling me to come back if it didn't get any better, I was relatively happy.

A week later my speech had become slurred and hesitant. I guess this is when the fear began to bite. As an academic, words were my trade, and, as anyone who knows me will tell you, I am quite a talker. I would be sitting in a meeting and would want to say something. I could hear the words clearly in my head but when they came out of my mouth it felt as if my mouth were not keeping up with my brain.

The next weekend I lost coordination of my right arm. Now not only could I not talk easily but I couldn't write or type properly either. I would sit in front of my computer with my nose nearly against the screen in order to be able to see, guiding my right arm with my left hand so as to be able to hit the keys in order to type. And, just to make life really fun, my balance continued to get worse. One of the nastiest symptoms I had was vertigo which was made much worse by bending my head forwards. I couldn't even wash my hair without the world spinning and I would end up throwing up. If you ever have a choice in the matter, which of course you won't, I would advise you not to opt for vertigo.

Once again I went back to Dr Wilson who seemed to be of the opinion that it was a severe inner ear problem. As it was my right eye and my right arm that were affected and my speech was slurred, I was beginning to have a suspicion that I might have had a stroke. At my request he agreed to send me to a specialist. I was assuming he would send me to an ear, nose and throat specialist. I had been waiting each morning for the post in the hope that I would receive the appointment. It finally arrived and I opened the envelope hoping that the appointment would be very soon. The first thing I saw was the letter heading from a unit for Neurology and Neurosurgery! I completely freaked out at seeing the word Neurosurgery. My immediate thought was, "Shit, I'm right . . . I've had a stroke." What were they going to do, for goodness sake? Cut my head open? I sat there reading the brief letter over and over again with the word "neurosurgery" echoing round my brain. The other thing that upset me was that the appointment was not for another five weeks. I began to panic. If I was being sent to a neurologist then I must have something really wrong with me. I rang the hospital that day to see if I could get an earlier appointment but was told that the one I had been offered was the earliest they had. I had no choice but to grit my teeth and count down the days.

At this time a friend of mine, Charlie, was doing some work with me at the office. We were sitting in front of my computer putting some data into a spreadsheet one afternoon; Charlie was reading out the numbers and I was typing them in on the computer. Well, there I was peering at the screen and not being able to see very clearly at all, guiding my right hand with my left to try to hit the keys (mostly a case of third time lucky) and talking to my friend while working. As the afternoon wore on she started worrying about how slurred my speech was getting. She had read out a number to me and I said, "Can you say that one again Charlie?" as I had had to on several occasions. She frowned and said, "You are talking really badly Cari." I shrugged and brushed it off. A few minutes later I said something else to her and she said, "Look, I am getting scared at the rate your speech is deteriorating, Will you *please* go and see a doctor this afternoon." I guess I'd been getting used to slurring.

I already knew that there was no chance of getting to see Dr Wilson within the next three or four days as his list was always fully booked in advance. I remembered that, as a member of staff at the University of London, I had access to the University Health Centre without being a registered patient. So, I rang the Health Centre and they told me I could turn up at the emergency clinic in an hour's time.

I felt that I would have quite a lot of trouble talking clearly enough to tell a new doctor what had been going on over the last two or three weeks so, before I left the office, I laboriously typed out a record of what had happened since 12 October. I was seen by a really nice GP, Ray, who was very kind and gentle with me and who read the record I had taken with me. He sat patiently and maintained eye contact with me the whole time I was talking. Every so often he would nod and smile to indicate that he was listening. He asked sensible questions and seemed to really listen to my responses and to take what I was saying seriously. He offered comments and told me what he was thinking might be going on with me. In other words he communicated with me. He was also very sympathetic. He then took me into an examination room and ran through all the same tests as Dr Wilson had but he told me after each test what he observed: "You are a bit wobbly . . . you have trouble making your arms go where you want them to . . . your legs are not terribly well coordinated" etc. I felt as if I was being taken seriously, which simultaneously reassured and scared me.

He eventually said that he thought it *might* be an atypical migraine given my past history of them but was concerned enough to send me straight to the Accident and Emergency Department of a local hospital. As I was leaving he said, "Come back and tell me what they say, OK?" I arrived at the hospital with a letter from Ray asking them to see me and, presumably, describing the symptoms that caused him concern. I rang my boyfriend, Luke, from the hospital to tell him I was there and explained that I would let him know later what happened. I was called in almost immediately. The nurse asked me what was wrong, how long it had been going on, whether I had seen my GP or not and took my pulse and temperature. She then asked me to get undressed and to put on the hospital gown and to lie down on the trolley until a doctor came to see me. I spent three and a half hours lying on that trolley behind closed screens in the accident and emergency area and listening to other people being treated. Most people seemed to be there because they had stubbed a toe a week ago, or had had a sore throat for two weeks and had not been to see their GPs or other trivial complaints. An elderly man had been admitted suffering from bladder retention (as far as I could ascertain from overhearing conversations). He was yelling and carrying on and generally causing chaos. The nurses and doctors were doing their best to calm him down and finally decided to catheterise him to relieve his bladder. At that point all hell let loose. He screamed and shrieked every time they went near him. This went on for some time until I heard the nurses tell him to shut up and lie still. Everything went quiet and a few minutes later I heard him let out a blissful sigh of relief.

By this time four hours had gone by and it was nearly ten o'clock at night. I had still not been seen by anyone and there seemed little hope that I ever would be as the place was getting busier by the minute. Finally, feeling scared and tearful, I gave up, got dressed and went home. As I left the cubicle, a male nurse was walking past so I stopped him and told him that I was leaving. He tried to convince me, rather half-heartedly, to stay but finally shrugged and said "OK. but its your decision." I left UCH and went and rang Luke to tell him that the whole event had been pointless. We went out to dinner and talked about what might be wrong with me, but neither of us could guess. I told Luke that I was not going to bother to go back to see a GP and that I had decided to wait for my appointment at the neurology hospital. He was very concerned about me by that time but agreed that it was probably the best plan of action. After seven weeks of continuing deterioration on all fronts and getting more and more scared about what was happening to me I was seen in the outpatient clinic at the unit for Neurology and Neurosurgery.

So it was at ten o'clock on a Monday morning in November 1992 that I arrived at the hospital with my sister Viki, who had taken the day off work to come with me. We sat in the waiting room talking generally about what they might find and do. Every so often a nurse would come over a sit and chat to us for a while. I guess they are used to people being scared at turning up at the hospital for the first time. I was finally called and decided to go in to see the doctor on my own. I went into a small consulting room where a rather good-looking registrar, Chris, was waiting for me.

Chris was what most people would describe as "classically" handsome. He was young, clean-cut and smart and wasn't wearing the normal doctor's white coat. He asked me to tell him what had been going on, how and when the problems had started and how I was at that moment. He ran through the same tests that Dr Wilson and Ray had done. In addition he checked my ability to feel pin-pricks over my body and checked if I could tell whether he was bending my big toes up or down when I had my eyes closed. He then asked me to get dressed and went back to his desk.

I emerged from behind the screen thinking that he would say it was something trivial. I sat down and he said, "I don't want to scare you, but I'd like to admit you to the ward immediately." Needless to say I was both shocked and scared. "Do I have to come in?" I asked. He said, "Well, we *could* do the tests through outpatients but it would take a long time and I really do think you should be admitted now for a week or so." He then very slowly reached out and picked up the phone and, while looking at me, gently said, "I'm going to ring the ward now to arrange it . . . OK?" I gulped audibly and said nothing. Actually I was on the verge of tears and didn't trust myself to open my mouth to respond to him. I was so shocked that I was not even capable of asking him what he thought might be wrong with me. He rang the ward and then turned to me and asked, "Have you got someone with you?" I nodded and he said, "OK. Why don't you go and sit in the waiting room and someone will come and take you up to the ward."

I walked back to the waiting room in a daze and sat down next to Viki. She asked me what the doctor had said and I told her that I had to be admitted to the hospital straight away. I was still playing the game that it was no big deal and that I could handle it. After ten minutes or so a business-like nurse, Yvette, turned up to take me to the ward. The first thing I had to fill in an admission form, and, as I could not write Viki filled in the form with me. When I got to my bed on the ward I realised that, of course, I had no night clothes or books or anything with me so I asked if we could go back to my flat and come back in an hour's time. Yvette hmmm'd and aahhhh'd a bit but finally said that it would be alright, so Viki and I went back to my flat and had a sandwich. I quickly threw a few things into a bag and went back to the hospital an hour later. Viki left to go home and I sat on my bed feeling a bit lost and waiting for something to happen. At about three o'clock the registrar, Chris, who had admitted me that morning, turned up and took down my medical case history, ran through all the tests again even more thoroughly and wrote down his observations in my notes. He seemed rather weary and distracted so I said, "Had a hard day have you my dear?" to which he replied, "Yeah, its all these damned patients." I then asked him what was likely to happen while I was in the hospital. He replied, in a rather matter-of-fact way, "You'll have an MRI and some other tests and, of course, a lumbar puncture." I looked up sharply and said "What? Do I *have* to have one of those?" He nodded and replied "Yeah, everyone at this hospital has a lumbar puncture, it's one of the perks of being here. You'd feel hard done by if you didn't get one."

Yvette then came back and went through the ward admission form with me. She wanted to know all about any other illnesses I had (I wanted to ask "Other than what?"), if I had any dietary restrictions (I was allergic to milk and butter) and what physical problems I had at the moment. At the end of the interview she said with a smile, "You aren't at all worried about this are you Cari". I replied, "Look, I am freaking out right now OK? I am

36

fucking terrified." She seemed surprised and said "Really? But you seem so calm and are joking all the time!" I nodded and said, "Yeah, I know. Do me a favour hon, don't fall for the bluff OK? It's just my way of coping."

As the day wore on some of the other patients came over to my bed to say hello. They were very kind to me and understood, without me having to tell them, just how scared and alone I felt. I began to realise that there was a particular ethos on that ward. The patients all looked out for each other, calling a nurse or doctor when someone needed them and providing what support they could for each other. They made sure that I knew what time meals were served and where to go and that I had someone to sit next to and chat to. All in all they were wonderful. They also told me the most important thing . . . where I could go to smoke! We were all largely in the same boat as that ward was where people who were in for diagnosis were put.

The following afternoon I was called by a nurse to go upstairs and have visual, auditory and sensory evoked potential tests. This is where they stick electrodes all over your head and make you look at silly, moving geometric patterns on a computer screen to see if your brain is picking up the signals from your eyes at the normal speed. They then put a clip on your right hand and send electrical impulses through a muscle to make your thumb twitch to see if your brain is picking up the messages properly. Then they put headphones on you and make you listen to different bleep tones in alternate ears. The worst part of this was trying to get the gel which they used to attach the electrodes to my scalp out of my hair. As I was still suffering from vertigo I could not wash my hair, so I had to put up with having the equivalent of hair gel stuck in my hair for the rest of my time in the hospital.

I was desperately hoping that I would be able to leave the hospital by Thursday morning as I had to go to an international conference at work that I had spent the previous six months organising. I simply didn't know how it could run smoothly unless I was there to organise it on the day. I kept telling the nurses and doctors that I had to get back to work for Thursday. The most they ever said was, "Well. We'll see." I got the people at work to come to the hospital each day to update me on how the organisation of the conference was progressing and would send them away with lists of instructions. I was basically conducting my work from the ward.

The next thing I was subjected to was a lumbar puncture. Now, the weird thing is that for as long as I could remember I had always dreaded the thought of a spinal tap, even the words struck fear into my heart. This is strange because I had never had *any* reason at all to believe that I would ever have to have one. Anyway, the dreaded morning arrived. No one told me what to expect, except for the other patients, who all said it was no big deal, and I was not even given a sedative prior to this wonderful experience. That morning Robert, the Senior House Officer (SHO), had been doing the rounds and, as he was leaving my bedside, said "MS is quite common, you know". I freaked out and told him rather forcefully that I *did not* want to hear those bloody letters unless he had *some* evidence, which I knew that he hadn't got as none of the test results were back. I realise now that he had already guessed what was wrong with me. After all, I was the right age with the right symptoms.

Later that morning Robert came over to me and announced "OK, we're ready now." I was shaking like a leaf and, had I been physically able, would have run off the ward screaming. But I did what I was told. I had to lie on my side on my bed and curl into a foetal position. For anyone who has never tried it I can tell you that this is a position that makes you feel extremely vulnerable, a classic case of people doing things behind your back. Robert then started saying the typical "medico" things that now make me *mad*. "Just a little prick" that was the local anaesthetic going in three or four times and then, "You won't feel anything now . . . just a little push." However, I *did* feel the needle going in and a sharp pain shot down my leg and I flinched away from it. "Don't move!" he snapped at me "I can't do this if you flinch!" I gritted my teeth while muttering obscenities at him under my breath. Unfortunately this LP did not work, he got what he later told me was a "dry tap". In other words he could not get any cerebro spinal fluid out. So, we went through the whole process again, and again, and again.

When he said "Just a little prick" for the fifteenth time I looked over my shoulder and snapped at him, "Yes you are, aren't you!" The nurse, Amanda, who was with me got the giggles and Robert got a bit flustered. Finally he admitted defeat and called in a registrar, Andrew, to come and do it. As Robert was packing up the gear I told him I wanted to see the spinal needle he had been using. He looked totally shocked and said, "No, you don't want to see that!" I pointed out to him that, as I had spent an hour having the damned thing stuck in my back, I wanted to see what he had been doing. He grudgingly showed me the rather large spinal needle and I commented that I was surprised it wasn't even bigger. It both astounds and amuses me that doctors seem to think that patients ought to be able to cope with painful and distressing medical procedures but are not able to cope with information about what is being done to them or what is wrong with them. I have come to the conclusion that all medical students should be forced to undergo the same tests and procedures that they will subsequently subject their patients to.

After ten minutes Andrew, turned up and said, "Come on. Let's get this done." I took one look at Andrew and felt his bedside manner might perhaps leave something to be desired. He had the kind of face that seemed to be incapable of smiling. He told me that he would do the LP with me sitting up so the CSF could drain down to where he could get it. So I sat up and, having already gone through the experience, told him to let me brace my feet against the wall so that I didn't flinch. He shrugged and said, "Whatever." He put a pillow on my knees and told me to bend forward over it. He got the needle in first time and carefully supported my head while he laid me down on my side. Oh joy, it worked this time! If only he had been the person to do it in the first place. Finally, it was over and I was told to stay lying down for several hours and drink a lot of fluid to help prevent the classic post-LP headache. The other patients were great and came to my bedside with bottles of squash as all I had to drink was water. By early evening I was feeling OK and went downstairs to ring Luke and have a cigarette. As I was on the phone I started going hot and cold and felt a little sick, so I told Luke that I had better go before I passed out and went and sat down with some of the other patients who had gone down stairs to have a smoke. One of them looked at me and said that I had gone as white as a sheet and, jokingly, handed me the wastepaper basket we were using as an ashtray saying "Heh, you can be sick in this", which I promptly was. The funny part of this was handing the wastepaper basket to a passing nurse and asking her if she would like to do something with it.

The next day (the day of the international conference) I was told that I was going to have an MRI (Magnetic Resonance

Imaging) brain scan. Well, some of the patients on the ward told me that this was really nasty, that they had felt claustrophobic and the noise was intolerable. However, as I was feeling decidedly grotty after the lumbar puncture and had a blinding headache as a result of it, I didn't really care what anyone did to me any more. In the early afternoon I was taken down in a wheelchair to the scanner and was put inside a big metal tube (the MRI scanner) with my head strapped down to prevent me moving. The scan began and a matter of minutes later I had fallen asleep! Frankly I found the experience very soothing and relaxing. OK, so I'm weird.

No one had actually talked to me about what might be going on except for Robert, who had mentioned MS in passing. On the fourth day I was taken into a side room and was shown my MRI scan. Andrew and Robert pointed out that there was only one patch of inflammation and no problems anywhere else— that I had what I heard as, encephalitis (that just means inflammation on the brain), although when I challenged this some months later they claimed they had said encephalomyelitis (otherwise known as "yuppie flu"), and that it would go away and I would be fine.

The effects of the lumbar puncture were terrible and continued to get worse. The afternoon of the day after they had done it I was lying on my bed feeling rough when I started to get an appalling cramping pain in my neck and shoulder muscles. It got worse and worse in the space of a few minutes until I was eventually crying with the pain. Susan, the lady in the bed next to me, came over and asked "Are you OK, Cari?" Susan was suffering from Myasthenia Gravis, a condition in which the muscles fatigue very quickly, leading to problems with moving and breathing. I shook my head. She asked me if I wanted her to get a nurse and I cried harder and nodded as I was incapable of talking. Amanda, the nurse who had been with me during the LP debacle, came running over and asked me what was wrong. I liked Amanda as she always made time to chat to the patients and always had a joke or a kind word for people as she went about her business. She looked terribly young as she normally had her hair done in a long plait. She looked a bit like an athletic schoolgirl.

I managed to choke out that I had agonising pain in my neck and shoulders. She went away and came back quickly with some painkillers for me to take. This pain continued to get worse over the next day to the extent that I could not even sit up or eat and the nurses and doctors were getting worried about what was going on. They got a physiotherapist, Ann, to come and see me to check whether they had dislodged a vertebra during the LP but she could find nothing wrong. They gave me a heated pad to put behind my neck which helped to some extent to relieve the cramp.

As all the diagnostic tests had finished, I was being left pretty much on my own for long periods of time and was beginning to feel that they thought I was just being a nuisance. Finally on the Friday morning I was still in agony but, by then, all I wanted to do was to go home. Robert had arranged for me to see an occupational therapist, Carol, before I left the hospital so, on the Friday morning, I went downstairs to see her. She asked me about the physical problems I had and made a few suggestions about how she could make life a little easier. Things like using a non-slip sheet to put under paper to stop it slipping when I was writing and giving me a grip to put on pens so I had something more substantial to hold on to. I think she must have seen how tired and miserable I was because suddenly she said "Would you like a cup of coffee?". I asked her if it was, by any chance, real coffee or was it just instant. One of my great loves of my life is real coffee and the instant stuff in the hospital was vile. She said it was filter coffee and a few minutes later came back with a mug for me. I was sitting there sipping the coffee when she said "You've had just about as much as you can take this week haven't you Cari?" I nodded and started to cry. "I just want to go home now," I sobbed. "I think you should," Carol said, "I don't think it will do you much good to stay here any longer." I agreed wholeheartedly.

When I went back up to the ward Amanda came to me and said "Robert wondered if you would be prepared to take a tranquilliser to see if it will help." I said that frankly I would take *anything* to make the pain go away. She came back with a tablet which I duly swallowed. Unfortunately it had no effect whatsoever. I assumed that they thought I was hysterical or something and so I told Amanda that I wanted to go home. She asked me if there was anyone who could come and pick me up as there was no way I could walk home on my own, but there was no one that I could call who could get to the hospital until late that evening. Amanda went away but returned a few minutes later and said "I am going on my lunch break in ten minutes and I will walk you home OK?". I was somewhat embarrassed that I was putting her to so much trouble but was very grateful none the less. I packed up my bits and pieces and we left the hospital with Amanda carrying my bag for me. She took me all the way up to the door of my flat and I was thanking her for walking me home when she suddenly reached out and hugged me, kissed me on the cheek and said, "I'm so worried about you. Please take care of yourself. You know where we are if you need us. Just turn up on the ward." She was pretty special.

I spent the next two weeks recovering from the effects of the lumbar puncture. I had had migraines many times before but this pain was worse than anything I had ever imagined was possible. For two weeks I was unable even to lift my head off the pillow without the most blinding pain in my head that I had ever experienced and my neck and shoulder muscles going into spasm. Needless to say this was a pretty miserable time. I finally managed to get back to work but felt very fragile for a long time and, of course, for the first time encountered the never-ending stream of well-meaning inquiries about my health. I was cheerfully telling people that I had encephalitis and that I would be fine soon.

Between then and December my symptoms and general state deteriorated to the point where large parts of my body had gone numb and my balance was so bad that I could barely walk without assistance from a friend. As luck would have it, Luke took me away for a pre-Christmas weekend at a very luxurious country hotel. My balance was pretty bad by then so walking around in the country was not exactly my favourite pastime. However, I managed to get about a little by hanging on to his arm for support. Well, we had a wonderful meal in the hotel that evening (wine and candlelight—all very romantic) and then went up to our room to go to bed. Needless to say, we started to make love when I realised with horror that I couldn't feel anything! All sensation below my waist had gone. I cried for ages, partly through misery but mostly through fear. How Luke managed to hide his distress from me I will never know. Throughout the whole episode he managed to be the strong one. He never drew attention to the problems I was experiencing but was always there for me. He never asked me about how I was feeling but was ready to talk when I needed to. He was simply amazing.

I returned to London the next day and after a couple of days more, with larger parts of me going dead I called out Dr Wilson. When I opened the door it was not him but a doctor I had never seen before. The locum, Paul, heard what I had to say about my physical state and the rate of deterioration, took one look at me and said, "Time for steroids I think". Paul was quite a character. He was tall and well-built, but was rather eccentric as he wore a full length cape.

Having been on steroids for a time when I was a child suffering from an undiagnosed lung condition I knew what they could do to you in terms of weight gain and acne and told him I really did not want to be on them again. He firmly but gently maintained that it was necessary now and that intravenous steroids often do not have the same side-effects as tablets. I was feeling more scared and upset all the time and when he looked at me in silence for a moment and then said gently, "This is really scary isn't it?", I burst into tears. He was one of the first people to verbally acknowledge my fear and it completely undid me. "I don't know what's going on," I sobbed "What the hell is happening to me?" "Don't worry," Paul said "We'll get you on steroids and sort you out."

He rang the hospital from my flat and said to the registrar, Chris, who had first admitted me "Cari Loder, demyelinating disease, acute exacerbation, needs steroids I think" he nodded once or twice and then put the phone down and told me that I should go to the hospital immediately to be admitted. Knowing what I now know about MS (that it is a demyelinating disease) I realise that he did indeed know that the diagnosis was MS, but I guess he assumed that I would not know what he was talking about on the phone—which of course was true. As soon as he left, I rang my sister-in-law, Hilary, to tell her that I was going into hospital again. As it was just before Christmas, my mother was staying with them and I heard her in the background asking Hilary what was wrong. I heard Hilary say "Cari has to go into hospital again. She has got worse." I then heard Simon say, "Auntie will be here for Christmas won't she?" Hilary told him that she wasn't sure but that they would come and visit me anyway. I was close to tears so when Hilary said, "God bless, we will all be thinking of you" I started to cry and put the phone down. I then rang a colleague at work, Heather, to ask her if she would come and walk to the hospital with me to help carry my bag as I could not manage on my own, which she did, bless her.

So, I was in the hospital four days before Christmas for a course of intravenous steroids (1 gram a day for three days). This was my first encounter with Venflons (the drip needles) and intravenous drips. I got out of the hospital the day before Christmas Eve, feeling pretty rough, partly due to the symptoms and the fact that the steroids left a ghastly taste in my mouth and made me very hyper and, at the same time, very depressed. On Christmas Eve my father drove me out to Hilary and Clive's where I was going to spend Christmas with the family. I spent much of the Christmas holiday lying down on my own and crying through sheer misery and fear. I still had no real idea what was happening to me. What is more, this was the first time that most of my family had seen me since all this had started and I could see that they were pretty worried about me, which in turn upset me even more. My eldest niece and nephew, Mari and Simon, in particular were upset but were so kind and understanding that I felt I had to go out of my way to play it all down and make them feel that their Auntie was really all right. This need to make it better for others was something that I was going to deal with over and over again.

On Christmas morning Mari came up to the room I was staying in and sat quietly on the floor watching me trying to put my make-up on. I realised that, although she was quite worried, she did not feel able to ask what was wrong with me. As I struggled to control my hands and arms to put my lipstick on without it going all over my face, I began chatting to her. "You see," I said "I have to try *really* hard not to stick the lipstick up my nose!" I grinned at her and then said "Ta da! Success!" She giggled at me. I smiled at her and asked gently, "Are you scared about what's wrong with me, Mari?" She pondered that for a moment and then shrugged. That was typical of Mari. I went and sat down next to her and put my arm round her. "Listen kiddo," I said "I'm going to be fine. I'm not going to die. OK?" She smiled tearfully at me, nodded and hugged me and then ran off downstairs.

I returned home the day after Boxing Day feeling like death warmed up. It was during this time that I first felt suicidally depressed. As no one had told me about depression being a common side-effect of high-dose steroids I had no way of putting what I was feeling into perspective. I seriously considered killing myself. I even went as far as writing letters to leave for my family to explain why. As I was writing the letter to my eldest nephew, Simon, I realised that there was nothing I could say that would make it acceptable for him. The thought passed through my head that, where Simon was concerned, I couldn't live with myself if I killed myself. What a totally stupid thought! This was what saved me from committing suicide and became a strategy that kept me sane through the following two years. Seeing the ludicrous side of life.

However, over the Christmas break and a *lot* of rest I began to recover and showed a distinct improvement by early January. A few weeks later I went to the hospital outpatients' clinic on a standard follow-up and was astonished when the doctor started talking about how little the medical profession knew about MS. That was all very interesting but I didn't *have* MS, so what on earth was she talking about? This confusion went on for some time until I finally asked Paul if there was anything in the letters from the hospital that indicated I had MS? He sat in front of me apparently reading the letters and then looked up and said, "No, there is nothing here to suggest it is MS." I spent that evening with Luke celebrating the fact that I had been given the all-clear.

I requested more and more answers from the doctors at the hospital clinic and finally demanded to know from Brian, a new (to me) Senior House Officer on the clinic, why they now seemed so apparently convinced that I had MS. He rather brusquely opened my notes and said, "Well, it's pretty clear. Multiple white matter lesions in both hemispheres, more prevalent infratentorially" (that means in the brainstem I later discovered). His report of my MRI scan in no way fitted with what I had been shown and told. He subsequently wrote to my GP saying:

I had a rather difficult interview with this lady talking about the diagnosis of MS that was made. She appears somewhat bitter that she was originally told that this was an encephalomyelitis and I have however explained to her that this seems entirely reasonable with the clinical presentation. (1 June 1993)

The problem was that I had still not been told officially that I had MS. Robert had mentioned it in passing before any of the test results were back and various SHOs at the clinic at mentioned MS but no one had actually said to me "You have MS." The problem was that my hospital notes said I had MS and the doctors seeing me quite reasonably assumed that I had been told. I subsequently found out that my sister Viki had been told that I had MS while I was in the hospital the first time and was under the quite reasonable impression that I had been told the same. This led to quite a few confrontations with my family who assumed that I was just "in denial" about the diagnosis. This made me mad as hell because I was *there* and I *knew* what I had been told. And, as far as I was concerned, I had *not* been told I had MS. This appears to have been the root of the problem. No one had told the SHOs, the registrars or my family that I had *not* told that I had MS.

In some ways the realisation that people I had trusted had treated me like a fool was almost harder to deal with than the dawning realisation that they were now saying I had MS. I became viciously, bloody angry with the medical profession and with the hospital in particular. At this point Paul left the practice, so I went to find a new practice and a new GP. I remembered Ray who had sent me to casualty that night in October 1992 and also by then realised that I ought to get some help from a counsellor, a service which he could arrange. I asked him if he would be prepared to take me on as his patient.

This was a significant turning point for me as I had found a superb doctor who was and still is incredibly supportive. However, by now it was July 1993 and I had endured nearly nine

months of confusion, terror and continuing physical deterioration. To put it in a nutshell, I was in one hell of a state, both
physically and emotionally. My legs were going weak and I was
dragging my right foot along the ground putting me in constant
imminent danger of tripping and falling over. It was around this
time that I actually fell on the street for the first time. My feet
were so numb that I couldn't keep my slip-on court shoes on and
one shoe flew off and I fell flat on my face. I didn't hurt myself
and managed to walk the rest of the way back to my office where
I sat down and cried for ages. In some way this really brought
home to me the enormity of what was happening to me. My
body was out of control. That was the last time for eleven
months that I was able to walk in anything but trainers.

When I knew Paul was leaving the practice and Ray had said
that he would take me on I asked Paul if I could have the letters
written by the hospital to give to Ray immediately to facilitate a
fast hand-over. Paul, who, as far as I was concerned at least, had
spent eight months telling me there was nothing in the letters to
suggest I had MS, promptly handed the letters over, not even
putting them in an envelope. He wished me well and said
goodbye. As I think anyone would have done, I started reading
the letters as I was walking down the street on my way back to
work. I think you can imagine my absolute shock and horror at
reading the discharge letter from my November 1992 stay which
was headed "Clinically Definite Multiple Sclerosis with Laboratory Support". Paul, who I had trusted implicitly and had liked
enormously, had been concealing the truth as well, and what
was worse, he had handed over the letters to me and must have
assumed I would read them. To this day I can not understand
how a doctor, who had spent many hours talking to me several

times each week and supporting me and, essentially counselling me, could be quite so unthinking. I felt totally betrayed.

What *still* makes me go into a rage is that all the doctors had all known for eight months that I had MS and not one of them had seen fit to tell me the truth clearly and openly. I had to find out the earth-shattering truth reading a letter while walking down the street. Wouldn't it have been so much kinder for them to have told me in an environment where I could have talked to someone and asked questions? As far as I knew MS were letters I saw on the side of collecting tins and all I knew about Multiple Sclerosis was the horrific images on the publicity campaign posters from the MS Society that were in the underground stations prior to that time (accompanied by the slogan "The MS Society, a hope in hell"). To me Multiple Sclerosis meant ending up in a wheelchair, end of story. As if that were not enough to panic about I knew nothing about the sight, sensory, bladder or bowel problems. I simply wasn't prepared for the experience, but then again, who is?

I still feel the rage of that time as I write this. I even went so far as to ask my consultant, Dr O'Connor, some months later why on earth the hospital lies to people about their diagnosis. He said that where that happens it is mainly because the diagnosis of MS is still a bit difficult in the early stages and also that the doctors feel totally impotent in giving someone the news that they have MS when they know full well there is very little they can do for them. I think it is true to say that most of us would rather be told the truth and deal with it than to be lied to. I believe that we are stronger than the doctors think. They may not be able to handle the reality of MS, but we, the sufferers have to. Maybe they should ask us whether we think we know or fear what is wrong with us—believe it or not some of us have guessed long before the doctors get to see us. We are the ones who have to deal with it and cope with it and carry on with our lives. If we can do it then surely they can too. Can you imagine how it felt? My body was betraying me by the day. I was losing my sight and my ability to walk, talk and write and the doctors were saying that there was nothing seriously wrong. Believe me, not knowing what is wrong when you are in that state is far harder than knowing the truth and being able to put a label on it, and read up about it, and talk to other people with it.

Finally, on the urging of a counsellor, Steve, who by then I was seeing regularly, I requested a meeting with my consultant neurologist, Dr O'Connor, who I had never previously met. My first impression of Dr O'Connor was that he was like a teddy-bear. He was not particularly tall but was solidly built. The most distinctive thing about him, however, was his grin. He never just smiled but always grinned and when he did it spread from ear to ear. It was what I refer to as a real "shit-eater" grin. I walked into the lecture theatre and looked around at the rows of doctors sitting there expectantly. Dr O'Connor greeted me and asked me to sit down on the chair in front of his desk. He then waved a hand at the other doctors and said, "Ignore them. They are just here to watch and learn."

After playing the poor little confused patient part and getting him to show me my MRI scan, explaining to me what it showed, I squared up to him, slapped both letters from the hospital down on the table in front of him and said "Would you like to tell me then which of those is correct?" I think he realised pretty quickly that I was very, very angry with the hospital. He was rather dumbfounded that I had copies of the hospital letters and asked me how I got them. I explained and also reminded him about the Patients' Charter which allows patients to see their medical records. He turned to the Senior House Officers and remarked, "Well this just goes to show we have to be careful what we put in writing." I turned to the doctors and said, "No, it shows that you have to be careful to tell people the full truth."

He then checked me over and was apparently horrified at the state I was in, that my arms and particularly my legs were so weak, and promptly arranged for me to have a five-day course of intravenous steroids. He was also kind enough to say I could go in as a day patient as I only lived just round the corner from the hospital. I guess he realised that I was so angry with the hospital that staying in would not be a good idea either for me or them. He was extremely indulgent of my rage and said that he would tell the ward that I would be up in ten minutes or so but in the meantime he gave me my hospital notes to take out to the coffee lounge to read (an unheard of experience) and gave me my MRI scans to take away with me, saying, "These are yours, you will take better care of them than the hospital will." His allowing me to read my notes was incredibly significant for me. He was telling me clearly that he was not going to withhold information from me, not even confidential hospital notes. He was the first doctor who had let me know that, no matter what, he was going to tell me the truth, and he has adhered to this ever since. He has certainly never pulled his punches with me.

The steroids helped almost immediately and by the end of the second day I was walking much better and was going round the ward showing off how well I was doing, even walking without the help of a stick. As the course of steroids came to an end I started asking if I could have another five days to try and put the MS into remission. The SHO, Brian, who was dealing with me that week, said he would talk to Dr O'Connor about it. I hung around until early evening one day to see my consultant who came by on ward rounds with his gaggle of SHOs. They all stood at the foot of my bed talking *about* me, not *to* me, and discussing what had been happening with me. Dr O'Connor finally addressed me and said, "Of course you can't have any more steroids. These are highly toxic drugs. You have had too much already." They then talked at some length about the fact that I should really go on holiday or take up a hobby or stay off work for a while, all of which I declined to consider. It felt as if they were doing no more than telling me to give up and accept the inevitable.

Brian wrote to Ray shortly after that meeting. He wrote:

We have explained to her the side effects of steroids, however, she is currently expressing the view that she does not care about the long term and is merely concerned with doing as well as she can here and now. I am not sure whether we are being quite forceful enough in explaining the potential acute side effects of high dose steroids. (16 July 1993)

Why does this make me angry? You may think Brian was being quite reasonable under the circumstances. The fact of the matter is that I knew perfectly well what risks I was running with having high-dose IV Methyl Prednisolone. I was fully aware that high-dose steroids could cause diabetes, osteoporosis (loss of bone density) and avascular necrosis (leading to hip replacements). But I had told them very clearly that I was prepared to take a *risk* with using the steroids but I was *not* prepared to live with the *certainty* of what the MS would do to me if left untreated. That I felt was my choice and my right. This consistent attitude of the medical profession that they know best and the patients views are not to be taken too seriously makes me hopping mad.

Obviously they have a professional obligation to ensure that we are making completely informed decisions . . . but I think that once they are assured of that, we should be allowed to choose.

So I left the hospital still none the wiser as to how I could make myself better. I felt impotent and out of control, a feeling that was a total anathema to me. I could not accept that this had me beaten. In fact my sister-in-law, Hilary, reminded me recently that I used to say in the early days, "OK, MS may be incurable but it has never had to deal with *me* before!" I laugh at this now as it amounted to nothing more than pure bravado at the time but it proved to be eerily prescient. A matter of days after the last dose of steroids I started to deteriorate again and it was only a couple of weeks before I was badly in trouble again.

Other people responded to the news that I had MS in different ways. These ranged from the most common, "My cousin has had MS for twenty years and is fine, you would never know there was anything wrong with her", through the unthinking, "I had a friend who got MS, she died three years later", and the disbelieving "Surely you mean 'ME' don't you?" to my all time favourite response from a professional colleague of mine, Lorna, who said "Oh shit, what a bummer!" That final response summed it up for me. You may well ask just what I wanted people to say. It is easier for me to tell you what I *didn't* want them to say. I didn't want them to be shocked or upset as I didn't want to have to make them feel better. I didn't want them to simply say they knew someone else with MS as all that did was to force me to sympathise with that person. Lorna's response was perfect, as far as I was concerned.

It was actually very hard for me to ignore or compartmentalise MS when it was, in effect, in my face constantly. The thing was that I felt I had to be polite no matter what response I got and after a while that became terribly hard. There came a time when the depression and rage were at their worst that I just wanted to tell people to mind their own business and go to hell. I wanted to say, as mothers do to their children, "Think before you open your mouth."

As I said, I started to see Ray. He had remembered me from the previous November when he sent me to casualty, and had not been surprised to hear that I had been diagnosed with MS. He didn't hesitate to take me on as his patient despite the fact that a lot of GPs seem not to like to take on patients with MS as there is nothing they can do for us. After I had been seeing him for a while I asked him if he had thought I might have MS when he saw me the previous November, to which he replied that it had indeed been a possibility but was, at that stage, rather a long shot and that a less sinister explanation was more likely.

As soon as I had officially registered with Ray I told him that I thought it would be a good idea if I saw a counsellor as I had found myself talking about the MS to virtual strangers. I really *did* need to talk to someone in a legitimate context to prevent me from talking about it inappropriately. As I had been trained as a psychologist I was viewing this decision very dispassionately as the "sensible" thing to do but was not acknowledging that I actually needed help. As far as I was concerned I was going to cope and I didn't need anyone else to help me. In fact the idea of letting anyone else help me was more than I could contemplate. I always have been ludicrously independent.

Ray told me that he thought it was a very good idea and that he would find the right person for me but that it would take a couple of weeks to set it up. He then looked at me and said, "Don't worry, we will hang on to you in the meantime, we won't let you go under." He was as good as his word and saw me every week just to let me talk and to get me to start to unpack some of my feelings about what I was going through. This was very hard for me as rage at the hospital was my overwhelming response to the MS at that time and was, to some extent, a way of protecting myself from dealing with the much scarier feelings. The rage blanketed out any other emotional response. I simply had not allowed myself to get in touch with any of the feelings of loss, sadness, misery or fear.

He gently started to chip away at the defences I had built up and it was not long before I dissolved into tears in his office sobbing, "I *miss* me, I want me back!" This was the first thing I was able to acknowledge, that I was mourning the loss of my previous self. Not just the physical self but it felt as if I had lost many of the things that defined me. I could no longer work the way I used to, getting to the office early in the morning, working late in the evening and working at the weekends and, therefore, achieving a lot. I simply did not have the stamina to do it as I was sleeping for hours during the day due to the MS induced fatigue. Also, the rage I was experiencing had altered my behaviour and was getting me into quite serious trouble at work where I would bite people's heads off for no apparent reason, and as I believed I had no future in my career, I ceased to care about the consequences of my actions. As a result of all this going on and the realisation that my future was looking pretty bleak, I had also come to the conclusion that everything I had worked for over the previous years had all been for nothing. This left me adrift with nothing apparently to work for and, therefore, little motivation to do anything.

I guess the fact that I was constantly talking about my diagnosis of MS was really quite healthy; at least I was admitting it and trying to make it part of me, although it has to be said that most of what I said was about the hospital and my rage with the doctors. But I also realised that I was turning the experiences into a story, almost like a stand-up comedy act! The more I told my story the less emotional impact it had on me. It also reinforced my ability to see the ludicrous side of the whole thing which, as I have said, is what kept me sane. I discovered that I could make people laugh at my experiences. This again was significant. I was turning a horrible, terrifying experience into something quite positive. People *wanted* to hear my story, they seemed to enjoy it. Many people knew nothing at all about MS, but virtually all of them knew someone with MS, so hearing about what it was, how it affected me and how I tried to deal with it allowed them to understand their friends better.

By this time, due to reading and researching, I knew nearly as much about MS as my doctors did, and in some cases, I knew even more than them. It came as a bit of a shock to discover that many people I got to know who had had MS for a long time knew very little about the disease. I couldn't understand this as I felt a compelling urge to understand everything I could about this horror that had become a part of my life. You can't see what is happening inside your brain, so I *had* to be able to picture it and make some kind of sense of it all. I quickly outgrew the self-help books as I felt that half of what they were telling me was untrue at worst and trivial at best. So, I turned to the medical books and starting reading post-graduate medical text books and the reference books that senior house officers use all the time. My favourite one was the *Oxford Handbook of Clinical Medicine*. Whenever your doctor excuses himself from your hospital bedside for a moment he is often slipping behind a curtain to consult it.

This was a major breakthrough for me. Now I knew

something about what the medics knew and, more importantly, how they conceptualised MS, how they were taught to deal with patients with MS. I was able to play them at their own game. At last I felt as if I had some ammunition to fight this MS beast with. Once again I was, at least partially, in a position of power. I was no longer at the mercy of the medics at the hospital, I didn't have to take what they said as gospel, I could argue with them from a position of knowledge. Dr O'Connor was brilliant. Here I was arguing with him about treatment, debating with him the relative importance of my symptoms, telling him about a new drug in the States that I had heard about over the computer Internet, and he took it all in his stride and treated me as an equal. I had also taught myself how to do the neurological tests and was checking myself every day so, when I went to see him, I was able to tell him exactly what had happened since I last saw him and what the situation was which he would then recheck and confirm. Talk about patient power!

Then came the day when I had my first appointment with my counsellor, Steve. I wasn't really sure by then whether I wanted to see him or not but I went along to the appointment nonetheless. I had been sitting in the corridor outside his office for about ten minutes when he came and called me in.

I sat down and he asked me to tell him about what had been going on. So, I told him about the start and the diagnosis at the hospital and all the concealment and the way I found out that I had MS, in fact everything you have just read. I told it all very dispassionately and calmly, just a series of facts, but nothing about how I felt or was reacting to having MS. I guess I was still trying to show that I could cope perfectly well and the last thing I was going to do was to admit to a total stranger that I was having problems. Anyway, Steve then asked me about how I felt, and what having MS meant to me and how it had affected me psychologically. I started off telling him about the all-consuming rage I felt, both at the hospital and at MS, and ended up saying that I felt very alone and under enormous pressure to take control of the disease as no one else seemed to be prepared to do that.

Now we were getting to the heart of it, this was the really scary stuff. I didn't want to acknowledge these things let alone deal with them and I *certainly* didn't feel comfortable baring my soul to a stranger like this. I was used to being strong and hated the idea of being seen as weak. He looked at me and said "You want someone to look after you don't you?" to which I replied "NO! no way! I don't want to have to rely on anyone!" and I meant it. The idea of relying on other people and becoming dependent on others was for me the ultimate horror. He probed further; why I was so against being helped when it was so obvious that I needed support? So, the next time he said "You need someone to help you, to share the burden", I nodded and started sobbing. Well, that was it. It had taken him all of thirty minutes to crack the defences and open the floodgates.

From then on I saw him for an hour each week and spent much of each session crying uncontrollably. It was so important to me that I finally had someone there to support me and to validate and legitimise the way I was feeling. Someone I could rage at or cry with and who wasn't involved so I did not have to look out for their feelings. He told me that this was my safe place for an hour each week, a place where I could do or say anything, a place where I could take off the mask of coping. He was my lifeline right then.

Keeping the mask on, as I came to think of it, was one of the greatest pressures on me. Understandably, people at work were constantly asking me how I was and, given the trouble I was having walking, there was no way I could hide it from them. People who had not heard about the diagnosis would ask me why I was having trouble walking, or if they knew I had MS would ask me how I was doing. Not the social "How are you?" but the almost painfully sincere and very well-meaning "No, really, how *are* you?" I found myself telling them the truth in a light-hearted way and then, seeing the look of shock on their faces, or hearing their response of "Oh, I am *so* sorry", laughing it off and making it better for them. My classic response was "Heh, it's OK. It's not that bad you know. It's quite funny sometimes actually." They would go away apparently feeling quite relaxed about it, and I would go back into my office, close the door, and spend half an hour crying my eyes out. I have never felt so alone in my whole life.

Firstly I tried to get hold of as much information about the illness as I could on the basis that knowledge is power and, as the TV car commercial says, "You conquer fear through knowledge", besides which I am a researcher and wanting to find things out and understand them is an occupational hazard for me. This was a useful venture up to a point but initially I scared myself witless reading about what might be awaiting me down the line (incontinence? blindness? oh please . . . not that) and at first it actually raised more questions than it answered. Secondly I got very, very depressed and inordinately sad about the whole thing. I spent much of that time in mourning for the Cari that was before MS hit. I missed her and wanted her back. And lastly I found that it was impossible for me to believe it. I would regularly wake up in the early hours of the morning in tears and think "MS? . . . . *me*?? . . . gimme a break! . . . this *has* to be a mistake." I just could not reconcile the disease with me. It couldn't be true . . . it *mustn't* be true. It was at three o'clock one morning when I had woken up and was listening to the radio that I heard a song by Four Non Blondes for the first time. I lay there listening to the words and found myself crying uncontrollably. The words were about crying in bed, just to get the feelings out of your head, waking up in the morning and going outside and screaming at the top of your lungs "What's going on!" That became my theme song for a long time and, even now, when I hear it on the radio, it makes me tearful, as it takes me back to the way I used to feel in those bleak hours before dawn.

I truly thought that nothing could be worse than what I was going through then but I soon discovered that the worst was yet to come. There came a time when I would look back at this period and would have given anything to be where I was at this stage. I guess everything is relative.

During the course of steroids I had been staying at the hospital all day because I had met up with a group of women on the ward who had MS. They were the first people I had ever known who had MS and certainly the only people I had been able to talk to about it since I was diagnosed. I was getting into the lift one day on my way out of the hospital when a lady, Angie, in a wheelchair, got into the lift with me, looked at me and said "Have you got MS?" I was a little taken aback but told her that yes, I did and asked if she had it as well, which she did. We ended up sitting in the entrance hall of the hospital for four hours smoking and talking about MS, what it had done to us, how it affected our lives, what we thought of the medical profession, and (a taboo subject for the doctors which had both of us in fits of giggles) how it affected our sex lives ("Cari, don't you think sex is ghastly when you can't feel anything?" OH YES!) I cannot begin to explain how incredibly important this was for me. I finally had someone to talk to about what was happening to me who actually understood what I was talking about. From that day on I started spending whole days at the hospital talking to all the women in the hospital who had MS. As we all smoked we would spend a lot of time sitting in the entrance hall, which was the only place where we were allowed to smoke, talking. We set up a kind of self-support group of smoking MSers.

Word spread around the hospital that there was a group of people sitting in the entrance hall from early morning to late evening, only returning to the wards for meals or treatment (when the nurses would lean over the banisters and yell for a patient to come back to the ward), talking, smoking, howling with laughter and crying in each others arms. Before long we had about ten men, women and children between the ages of 12 and 65 turning up every day and the self-support group had been formed.

Looking back on that time in July 1993 it is hard to remember exactly how the group evolved. We went from two people talking about their experiences of MS, to a group of people of all ages with different illnesses supporting each other, swopping tips on coping with things and sharing feelings and fears, in the space of five days. It was not long before some of the nurses started to realise that the support this group was giving people was rather important and would tell new patients about it and suggest they come down and join us. So, the group just grew and grew. I felt calmer and safer at that time than I had since October 1992 when the illness had first started. I was no longer alone with the illness and when I was with these people in the hospital I no longer felt like a freak the way I did when I was outside in the "real world". That was the one place where having a disability made me 'normal'. It was the able bodied in the hospital who were the outsiders, the freaks. The hospital became my sanctuary.

I kept going back to the hospital after my course of steroids had ended just to have the support of the other patients there. One day when we were sitting in the day room next to the ward one of the nurses came up to me and told me that an SHO, Dean, on the ward, was annoyed at me for being there. I was frankly livid. This was an SHO who had never dealt with me before and I was furious that he should form a view as to whether I should be there or not. I also felt very extremely threatened by the thought that anyone could take my support group away from me. I asked the nurse to point him out to me. He was a tall, well-built, youngish doctor with blond, curly hair. A few minutes later I saw him come out of the ward and walked up to him and told him that I had heard that he did not approve of me being there and asked him just what the problem was. He started telling me that I should be at home resting and not hanging around at the hospital. I explained to him that I only lived a few minutes' walk around the corner and I was not travelling or anything. He said that he knew that but that I should still not be there.

I told him that being with the other patients was really helping me cope and that, despite appearances to the contrary, I was not handling the MS stuff very well. Dean then put his hand on my shoulder, leaned close to me and said very quietly, "It's OK Cari, I can see now, you're dying inside." I couldn't believe what I was hearing. This total stranger was the first doctor at the hospital who had even acknowledged the emotional side of MS, let alone been able to see what I was going through. And he cared about me. A total stranger who, as far as I was concerned, had no involvement in my case, cared enough to look out for my welfare. From that day on he always acknowledged me when he saw me, or joked with me, and in due course he became the SHO who treated me. He really was a very special doctor, a very special person.

My relationship with the doctors at the hospital changed radically over the next year, moving from one of complete hostility, to one of mutual cooperation. Dr O'Connor started seeing me in teaching sessions for the senior house officers and registrars where he would ask me to introduce my case history to them. I had to tell them about the symptoms I had first that led to me being admitted to the hospital, the tests that were conducted and the results, and what my physical situation was at the time they saw me. As I am a lecturer and am used to making presentations at conferences, the experience of performing in front of the medical audience held no horrors for me. In fact I rather enjoyed it. I considered it quite an achievement to be able to make the audience laugh out loud by teasing my consultant in front of them, which he responded to by teasing me back. At the end of one session a doctor who had been in the teaching session came up to me in the corridor as I was leaving and announced that my consultant and I had been dubbed the Cannon and Ball of the hospital! A comic duo of medical pathology.

As the SHOs on my consultants' team (or firm as they refer to it in the hospital) rotated every four or five months I was constantly having to deal with new doctors for getting my intravenous steroids, which by October 1993, I was having every two weeks. My consultant did me the unique courtesy of personally introducing me to each me doctor I would have to deal with, explaining to them in front of me, that I was very good at monitoring my own symptoms and that they were not to double check me or deny me steroids when I told them that I needed the treatment. One introduction cracked me up. The SHO was summoned to the consulting room where I had been seeing Dr O'Connor. Dr O'Connor then sat there for about twenty minutes telling the SHO that I knew exactly what I was doing, that other SHOs had been troublesome because they insisted on treating me as a patient, that I was "a very special patient" and that he must listen to what I was saying and on no account stop me doing what I wanted. I ended up feeling very sorry for the poor boy. He must have thought he had just been delivered the patient from hell!

Shortly after that I was given a young Senior House Officer, Mark, who had only just joined the hospital. Unfortunately he was rather clumsy and repeatedly failed to be able to put a needle in my vein for the intravenous drip, would leave the ward in a flustered state and would not return for some time. The next time I saw Dr O'Connor I told him that I did not want this particular SHO to do the IVs anymore as he seemed incapable of doing it correctly. Dr O'Connor then asked me if I would teach his new SHO how to do it properly! By this time I had access to the *Oxford Handbook of Clinical Medicine* and had read up the correct procedure for putting a Venflon in (the intravenous drip needle).

The next time that I had to have steroids and Mark turned up I told him in no uncertain terms that he could not put the Venflon in for me and to go and get a colleague to do it. He rather shamefacedly told me that he had been told that he must do it himself. I decided there and then that I would try and teach him his own trade. The first thing I refused to let him do was to use his stethoscope tied round my arm as a tourniquet. Apart from the fact that it did not work at all well as a tourniquet it was also rather uncomfortable as it pinched the skin. I rounded on him and said, "The first thing you can do is to drop that stupid affectation!" He once again looked rather forlorn and admitted that he did not have a tourniquet of his own and none of the other doctors would lend him theirs. I started to feel rather sorry for the youngster but said, "Oh for goodness sake. Use a blood pressure cuff instead." To give the lad his due he went straight off and got one and, of course, it worked perfectly well in terms of making the veins stand up.

I then helped him to identify the best vein to put the needle in (I was a bit of an expert on my own veins by then) and how to make sure it went in straight. All went well until he started to take the needle out, leaving the plastic catheter in, in preparation for linking it up to the drip bag containing the steroids. I immediately said to him, "Take the pressure cuff off first." He was panicking a little and got rather flustered and so ignored me. I knew perfectly well what was going to happen if he took the needle out while the pressure cuff was pumped up. He went ahead and took the needle out and, as I had predicted, blood spurted everywhere. It went all over his arms, on the bed and over me. I finally gave in and ripped the pressure cuff off myself to avoid any further mess.

I then sat him down and had a quiet talk about the way to do things. I am amazed that Mark didn't lose his temper with me given the way I was talking to him. He sat there with his hands in his lap and his head bowed like a schoolboy being told off by the headmistress. Far from losing his temper with me, what he did was to ask me if I knew where he could buy a tourniquet from! I felt so sorry for him by then that I told him I would buy him one and bring it in the next time I had steroids. When I next saw him a couple of weeks later and delivered a Rolls-Royce version of a tourniquet he was absolutely thrilled and went so far as to ask me to show him how to use it properly the first time as he had never seen one quite like it before. I know now that my reaction to the doctors was just part and parcel of my inherent inability to be intimidated by authority, but also that it was essential for me to feel at least partly in control of what was happening to me. The fact that I was unable to control the MS had always deeply offended me. As far as I was concerned it was the first time in my life that I had met a situation that I could not control through logical thought and hard work.

Dean, on the other hand, had no problems in dealing with me. He would walk onto the ward and stand in the doorway until he spotted me and, pointing across the ward, would yell "There she is!" I will never forget one time when Dean arrived to set the drip up for me. The other doctors had always turned up with the proper equipment neatly laid out on a metal tray and with the drip stand to hang the bag of steroids on. Dean started to sort things out and then realised that he had left his tourniquet behind. "Tell you what Cari," he said "Use the other hand to tourniquet your arm will you?" I grinned and obliged. He put the needle in the back of my hand and then realised that he hadn't got the special tape to secure it with. He rummaged around in his white coat pocket and eventually pulled out a scruffy, screwed-up sticking plaster. He slapped it over the drip needle and stood back to examine his work. "Hmmm . . ." he said "Not exactly sterile but I think it will do." I giggled helplessly at his breach of medical procedure. He then connected the needle to the drip bag and realised that he had also forgotten to get a drip stand. "Any ideas?" he asked. "Well" I said, "there's a coat hanger on the curtain rail. How about using that?" "Good idea," Dean grinned and hung the steroid bag on the hanger. "This is a new one on me," I said giggling "I assume this is the Heath Robinson approach to medicine." Dean and I cracked up laughing and he whispered to me, "Don't let the nurses see this. They'll freak out!" He then told me to regulate the drip flow and wandered off.

An hour later the drip bag was empty and I was waiting for a nurse to come and take the needle out for me. I asked several times but half an hour later I was still hooked up. I finally lost patience and decided to take it out myself. I was faced with the dilemma of how to do it one-handed as you have to keep pressure on the hole where the needle is while you pull it out. I finally came up with the idea of putting my right thumb over the hole while using my first and second fingers to pull it out. It worked fine, so I wound up the gear and took it over to a nurse. When she heard that I had taken the drip out myself she was appalled, as not even junior nurses are allowed to do it. From then on I took the drip out myself each time until it reached the point where the SHOs would tell the nurses just to let me get on with it. I quite enjoyed having intravenous steroids from then on as, once again, I felt as if I was in control.

♦

CHAPTER THREE

I'm Not Waving, I'm
Drowning

♦

From the 12th October 1992, when MS struck, my weeks were charted by a story of progressive disablement but it was not until July 1993 that the deterioration really started to speed up.

It was in the July of 1993 that I first started falling over and hurting myself. The first thing I did was to dislocate my little toe. It was the morning of the day that I first went to see Dr O'Connor my neurologist at the hospital and I was stumbling around getting ready to go when Viki, who was going to the meeting with me, knocked on my front door. I went to answer the door and, in the process, caught my little toe on the corner of a wall as I was walking past (I didn't have my shoes or socks on yet) but because my feet were completely numb I didn't realise what I had done. So, I got ready, went to see my consultant and, after I had been given the first steroid drip in a five-day course, came back home. Ray had asked me to ring him to tell him how the meeting had gone, so I sat down on the floor and took my shoes and socks off and rang him. As I was talking to him I noticed what I thought was a smudge of dirt between my little toe and the next one and went to rub it with my finger, at which point my little toe fell over sideways! I told Ray what had just happened and said that it looked as if I had dislocated my toe. He asked me if I could move my toe to which I responded that I couldn't. He immediately said that I would have to get to the surgery where he would have to reduce it and relocate it for me. While he was saying that I had grabbed my toe, pulled it up and relocated it, which I told him. He was apparently rather dismayed at what I had done until I reminded him that I had no feeling whatsoever in my feet so it didn't hurt. This inability to feel pain struck me as an amusing bonus of having MS!

While I was visiting the hospital every day for a week of daily intravenous steroids I met a group of women on the ward who had MS. They were all using NHS wheelchairs which, at that hospital at least, were bright red. When I first got to know these women they referred to the wheelchairs as their "buggies", which I felt was rather demeaning. Babies go in buggies, not grown women. One day I took all of them out to the park which was just outside the hospital to let them escape from the hospital for a short while. They were having great fun racing down the ramps in the hospital on the way out seeing who could do it without crashing into the wall at the end of the ramp! As I stood and watched them, laughing at their antics and wondering if I could ever cope with being in a wheelchair the way they did, I suddenly thought that they were just like the athletes in the film

Chariots of Fire racing against the odds; and that, seeing as their wheelchairs were fire-engine red, why not call them that? So the group of "four wheeled MSers" were duly dubbed the Chariots of Fire which, incidentally, they loved.

These strong and funny women taught me so much about coping. They were all so much physically worse off than I was and had had MS for several years whereas I was still walking and had only had it for nine months, but they had found ways of dealing with it and staying sane and, most importantly, laughing at it. They helped me realise that no matter how distressing or unpleasant things got there was always a ludicrous side if you only looked for it.

I guess the best example of this is when Angie was having problems with bladder retention (she couldn't pee) a very common problem with MS, and was having to learn to self-catheterise. The poor thing was having real trouble with this but the nurses kept on and on at her several times a day to learn how to do it. She finally ended up in my arms crying her heart out about it. She was feeling totally emotionally exhausted and was being made to feel a failure. I knew there was little I could do in terms of offering practical advice as I had, thankfully, never had to learn to self-catheterise myself. However, I fell back on our rule which was to laugh at the bad things.

I looked at her and said "Heh . . . I have an idea! Get your lipstick and draw a bullseye round where the catheter has to go and then pretend you are playing darts!" She looked at me solemnly for a moment before it sank in and then threw back her head and howled with laughter. We spent the next hour or so giggling helplessly, imagining the nurses' faces were she to do this! The next day she greeted me with the news that she had self-catheterised successfully for the first time that morning. She told me that when the nurse came round to get her to try again she couldn't stop giggling thinking about what we had talked about the previous day, and the more the nurse asked her what was funny, the more she got the giggles. Consequently she was more relaxed and therefore succeeded. Laughing in the face of fear goes a long way towards banishing it. Apparently the nurse asked her why she had been able to do it this time but not before, to which my friend tells me she responded "It was Cari and her dartboard!" One rather puzzled nurse left the ward. This became something of an urban myth on the ward I believe.

During that week I got a reputation on the ward for giving Brian the SHO, who was dealing with me, a hard time. One day Angie and the other women on the ward were sitting around one of their beds. They were feeling low that day so I had found the results of a sex survey in a magazine that a friend had brought in for one of them. We were sitting there deciding if we fitted the profile of the respondents to the survey when Brian came up to get me for my steroid drip. Needless to say, there had been much hilarity going on about the survey so, when Brian came up to the bed and said "Cari, I am ready for you. When would you like me to stick it in for you?" the other women started to giggle. I deadpanned and, looking at him seriously, said "My goodness, that is the best offer I have had all week." The women collapsed in fits of giggles. Brian got flustered and said, "I can either do it now or after lunch, whichever you prefer". Once again I deadpanned and said, "Heh, I'm up for both if *you* can manage it" Brian then blushed furiously and literally ran off the ward. All of us lost control and screamed with laughter. One of the nurses who had overheard the exchange came over to me and said with a wide grin "Ooohhh, you are really naughty. Would you do that again please?"

Between August and October 1993 my symptoms were developing at a rate of knots, my legs were getting weaker and weaker and more spastic (tight muscles *hurt*), my balance was quite pathetic, large parts of my body were numb, I was experiencing both bladder and bowel incontinence and the fatigue was completely out of control to the extent that, although I was still going to work each day, I would quite often not make it there until midday and would have to leave by mid-afternoon to go back home to sleep again, needless to say I didn't get any work done. I was very lucky to be working as an academic at the Institute of Education. My bosses were amazing. They didn't put any pressure on me, or make me feel as if I was failing in my job. Most importantly, they didn't make me feel as if I had been sidelined either. I will remain eternally grateful to my immediate boss, Gareth Williams, and to the director and deputy director, Peter Newsam and Peter Mortimore, of the Institute during that time.

Despite the physical problems I was having I was still reasonably mobile but after nine months my legs became so weak and uncoordinated that I started to fall over. The first time I fell badly was one evening in my flat when I wanted to pick something up off the floor behind a coffee table. As I bent down to pick it up I lost my balance, my legs gave way and I fell, scraping the whole of my left side against the table. I ended up lying on the floor crying, not through the pain (I couldn't feel anything), but through the sheer misery of not being able to perform the simplest task. Every time something like that happened it made me realise, all over again, just how bad things were and how bleak the future was looking.

The second time I had a bad fall was on the street outside my block of flats carrying some shopping. Once again I lost my balance and, because I had no hands free to grab on to anything, I fell full length on the pavement. Two girls who were near by were really nice and ran to my aid and picked up my shopping for me, which had gone everywhere, while I tried to get to my feet. I made it half-way and then lost my balance and fell again. I felt totally humiliated. I finally made it to my feet and was thanking the girl who had stayed with me when she looked at me and asked "Do you have MS by any chance? Only my Mum does and she used to fall a lot." I found her spontaneity incredibly refreshing. There was no embarrassment on her part and, therefore, none on mine either. I was able to say that yes, I did indeed have MS and then went on to ask her how her Mum had coped with it. We chatted for a while about MS and coping and how it affected people with it. She then proceeded to carry my shopping all the way to my flat for me (it transpired she lived in the same block of flats) and left telling me that if I ever needed any help, then just ask. It was heartening to know that there really are some good samaritans in the world. If you ever see someone staggering and falling on the street please *don't* assume they are drunk, they too may have MS and they might need your help. Bear in mind, it may be *you* in that situation some day.

I have encountered many people who would make a show of giving me a wide berth, presumably assuming I was drunk. One particular occasion upset me immensely. I was doing my best to walk as normally as I could but was, inevitably, weaving around. A lady was walking towards me holding the hand of her young child. As they drew nearer I saw her give me a sidelong glance and she pulled the child out into the road to walk past me, keeping as far away from me as possible. She obviously thought I was more of a risk to her child than the traffic was! I was both upset by their reaction and embarrassed that I could not walk normally. There were many occasions when I was reduced to tears while walking down the street. Every time something like that happened it slammed the reality of what was happening to me back at me again. It never seemed to get any easier to cope with. Partly that was my fault as I was determined not to "get used" to having MS. I felt that if I accepted it then I would give up and would stop fighting. I reckoned that, as long as I could fight, I stood a chance of beating it and getting back to the way I used to be. I was constantly looking for things to improve. If, even for a moment, a symptom eased a little I would be celebrating that the MS was going away. I don't know why but I always believed that I was going to get rid of MS. It was more than simple denial of reality. I truly believed that I would beat it.

I later got used to falling and stopped caring about what other people thought. After all, it was not my fault. One morning I had gone to a newsagents to get a magazine. The one I wanted was, as luck would have it, on the bottom shelf near the floor. I crouched down to get it (not a good idea as my thigh muscles were very weak by then) and promptly fell over and landed on my backside. I thought to myself "Oh dear, here we go again" and tried to struggle to my feet. I once again fell backwards. I sat there for a moment knowing full well what the other customers would be thinking. I started to feel upset and then thought "Damn them! I didn't ask for this!" I finally got to my feet and stumbled over to the till to pay for the magazine. As I neared the till I heard a woman behind me whisper to her friend, "It is disgusting that they are drunk this early in the morning." My blood boiled. I turned slowly round to face her and said, in my best "I am totally sober" voice, "I will do a deal with you my friend. You tell me what it is like to live with being a judgemental idiot and I will tell you what it is like to live with having Multiple Sclerosis." I am not sure that I had ever seen anyone blush quite so furiously in my life. I left the shop giggling to myself. Well, it made *me* feel better anyway!

One of the biggest lessons I learned from the experience of having MS was how to empathise with other people with disabilities. For the first time I realised just how offensive and upsetting well meaning behaviour and comments can be to the person with the disability. Things like constantly being offered help can feel incredibly undermining. Only being asked about how you feel or how you are coping can make you feel as if your whole life has been taken away. I think that it is fair to say that way most of us with disabilities would like to be treated is to feel free to ask for assistance when we want it and for it then to be offered. And for people to talk to us as intelligent individuals who have interests and concerns like everyone else beyond our physical situation. In other words, we want to be treated as normal people.

It was about this time that I had an appointment with my physiotherapist at the hospital. I had been seeing them from time to time for a few months, but there was not much they could do for me other than to teach me stretching exercises to try and keep the spasticity in my legs at bay. I turned up for my appointment to discover that my physio had moved elsewhere and that I would be seeing someone new. This was the physio, Ann, that had seen me on the ward after the lumbar puncture. As I was taking off my jeans and shoes, she started chatting to me. She obviously recognised me and said "Didn't I see you on the ward when you were in for diagnosis?" I told her that indeed she had dealt with me then. She then looked at me with a concerned expression and said, "I felt so sorry for you that day. You were in such appalling pain and we couldn't do anything for you." I was amazed as I had felt that they were just annoyed with me! It just shows that it pays not to jump to conclusions. Well, she checked me over and then told me she wanted to see me walk and, basically, was more than a little concerned about how unsafe I was on my feet. I was lurching and staggering and my right foot kept dropping down and tripping me up. The first thing she did was to fit me with a drop-foot orthosis (a piece of molded plastic that fits under your foot and goes up the back of your calf to keep the foot from flexing downwards). She then gave me two sticks to try to help with my walking but was not happy with that and finally gave me elbow crutches which I was much happier with, although she was still not convinced that I was really safe, and I had a bit of a battle with her to let me out of the hospital. I knew she thought I ought to be in a wheelchair but there was no way I was going to go down that route. She was also concerned that I was not due to see Dr O'Connor for another two months and said she would arrange for me to see him as quickly as she could as she thought he should really know what was going on. She was as good as her word and I got a letter from the hospital a few days later making an appointment for me to see Dr O'Connor the next week.

I was really glad to be using the crutches because they allowed me to walk more safely and for longer distances without getting quite so tired. But, of course, I started getting comments from total strangers in shops or in my block of flats who, when they saw me on crutches would say, normally with a smile, "What have you done to yourself then?" or "Been skiing have you?" At first I was polite and explained to them that I had an illness which made it difficult for me to walk. Then, as time wore on, I started to say that I had MS which was paralysing me, which as you can imagine, shocked them a bit. Finally I had had enough and when, at the end of a particularly tiring day, a woman in the lift with me said, with a broad smile on her face, "What have you done to yourself then?" I snapped, "I haven't fucking done anything, I have MS, it is paralysing me, want to know anything else?" I know it was cruel of me but I had had just about as much as I could take. The poor woman was very embarrassed and started apologising. She got very flustered and said, "I am so sorry. I didn't mean to offend you. How insensitive of me." I gritted my teeth waiting for her to tell me that she knew someone with MS but thankfully she didn't. Of course I immediately felt bad about the way I had reacted and explained to her that I wished I *had* done something to get in this state. That is what made me so angry about having MS. I had done *nothing* to get it. It was not my fault. There was nothing I could have done to avoid it and it appeared that there was nothing I could do to make it go away again. It was so damned unfair. And, to cap it all, I had to deal with the insensitivity, prejudice and fear of people.

I was forced to "go public" on my crutches only three days after I started to use them. It was my sister's one-year wedding anniversary and she was having a garden party to celebrate. I was finding it very difficult to use the crutches as both my legs but, more importantly, my arms would unpredictably go into spasms of pins and needles during which I could not move the limb that was affected. Using a particular limb could trigger the spasm within seconds. As you can imagine it was almost impossible to avoid a spasm when I was using my arms to lean on the crutches. All I could do was to stand perfectly still and ride the storm until it had passed. This led to a coping strategy of leaning against a convenient wall, smoking a cigarette and trying to look nonchalant until I could continue walking. This worked extremely well, except for the fact that it turned me into quite a heavy smoker!

My father and I arrived at the party and I struggled out of the car clutching onto my crutches for dear life. I was not looking forward to my family's reaction to me as this was the first time that would have seen me needing to use crutches to walk. As it happened they were fine and no one made a big deal about it, in fact my eldest niece, Mari, had great fun using the crutches to swing about on! All in all I felt quite comfortable about becoming a "four-legged" MSer. It was certainly preferable, as far as I was concerned, to becoming a machine on wheels, in other words, having to use a wheelchair. There were times when I felt that I simply had to get away and be on my own and this party was no exception. I was standing out by a field gazing into space and basically just taking time out. Although I was leaning on a fence to support myself, my legs would periodically give way under me and I would wobble a bit. I was sure that, although they were some way away, people would be looking at me and feeling sorry for me. That was the feeling I hated the most. I did not want people's sympathy. I did not want them watching me and making comments to each other behind my back, even well-meaning comments. I wanted to become invisible. I was fighting so hard to keep going that sympathy made me feel less than tough. All it would take was a few kind words and I would be reduced to tears. Hilary, my sister-in-law, finally came out to me as I was making my way inside to the toilet. She was obviously concerned and, as I walked past her, she stopped me by putting her hand on my shoulder and said "You mustn't give up, Cari. You have to keep fighting. You have got to be strong." I didn't want to hear that. I *was* fighting. I knew she meant it kindly but I was sick to death of people putting pressure on me.

Just how much more did they expect of me? Just how much more could I cope with? I wanted to scream, "I can't fight any longer. I have had enough. And what the hell am I fighting for anyway?" It made me tearful and I shrugged her off and went away to be on my own again.

There was one time, shortly after the party, when I could quite cheerfully have punched the woman in question although she had nothing but kind intentions. I was having lunch on a Thames river boat with my father who had been acting on behalf of the owners of the boat. As an additional thankyou to him they had invited him to bring a guest to have lunch on the river boat free of charge. Using crutches was still rather new to me and I had not yet fully mastered them so going up and down slopes to get from the dock to the boat was not the easiest thing in the world. However, I managed quite well and felt that I was doing a reasonable job of not looking too disabled.

We had just got on to the boat and the hosts invited us to sit with them to have a pre-lunch drink. My father was talking to the owner and I was sitting next to a female guest. I had just introduced myself to her when she leaned forward and said in a less than quiet voice, "How long have you been a cripple?" in the same tone of voice she might have used to say, "How long have you been a researcher?" I could not believe what I was hearing. This was a supposedly educated, intelligent woman. Regardless of being sensitive to people's feelings, had this woman never heard of political correctness? My gut reaction was to reply, "I have had MS for eleven months, how long have you been a moron?" Of course I didn't say that. What I actually said was, "If you are referring to the fact that I am using crutches, then I have been on them for two weeks. And I am not a cripple. I have a problem with walking at the moment because I have

MS." She still seemed oblivious of how offensive she had been but I let it go as I did not want to cause embarrassment to my father in front of his clients. I then played a game I had never tried before. I said, "Actually I prefer to refer to myself as 'differentially abled' or, if you prefer, 'ambulatorily challenged' ". She didn't quite know what to make of that! She had obviously not played the PC (political correctness) game before.

We sat down to have lunch with them and general conversation started. Predictably enough, people started asking me about the MS, how long I had had it and how it affected me. I was still not comfortable about talking about the illness but I tried my hardest to be polite to them when, suddenly, the woman started telling me that faith healing would cure me! I groaned inside realising that I was sitting opposite a religious enthusiast. When you have an incurable disease religious do-gooders seem to gravitate towards you. She talked on and on about how all I needed to do was believe I would get better, that I could cure the disease if only I believed etc. The only response I could trust myself to make without losing my temper with this insensitive stranger was to say, "It's a nice idea but I am afraid that MS is a little more complicated than that."

Luckily I was having severe problems with bladder incontinence at the time. I say luckily as it gave me the perfect reason to escape from them at regular intervals! Unfortunately we were dining downstairs in the boat and the toilets were upstairs at the other end of the boat. The stairs were very narrow and twisting and trying to negotiate them on crutches was no easy task. However, as always, I refused assistance and battled on. Several times on that trip I would realise abruptly that I needed to pee. The problem with MS bladder incontinence is that the second you feel you need to go is the second you *do* need to go. There is little or no warning. At the first sign it is already nearly too late. Anyway, I struggled up the stairs, negotiated the length of the boat and was feeling very happy to have reached the toilets in time. I was just opening the door to the toilet when suddenly I lost all control. I don't know if it is something psychological that lets you stop trying to retain control for a second because you know you have made it or what, but this happened to me on many occasions. I became very adept at managing to cope with the bladder incontinence. My obligatory uniform at that time was dark blue leggings as, because they are tight, nothing runs down your legs and the dark colour does not allow wet patches to show. And a long button-up jacket that further hides any evidence of an accident. I thought of it as my incontinence survival outfit!

The time I really did myself some damage was in my flat one night. I was getting ready to go to bed and, consequently, was not using my crutches as I could keep one hand on a wall at most times. I was walking about three feet from the wall to get into bed and, in the process, lost my balance, my legs gave way and I fell. As I fell I hit my side on the metal arm of a chair, which was fine by me as I couldn't feel anything as my body was numb from mid chest down, so I got back up and went to bed. In the morning I got up and put on my jeans and as I bent down to do my shoelaces up I noticed that my right side hurt where my jeans belt dug in. I prodded the rib where the pain seemed to be and wondered if I had bruised it or something. That day I was going to the hospital for my steroids and while I was there I mentioned to Dean, the SHO, that I had fallen and that my right side hurt a little bit. He took a look at it, prodded me and grinned and said "You've broken a rib. That will hurt like hell for weeks!" Needless to say I had no need to take any painkillers because I couldn't feel any pain at all unless I prodded the rib. It was not until five weeks later when I was sitting on the floor watching television one Saturday and leaned forward to pick up a magazine that I was hit by the most agonising pain in my side. So *that's* what a broken rib feels like, I thought. The fact was that those particular nerves had chosen that moment to come back to life again. I always said that MS was a contrary disease.

Probably the most potentially distressing thing I had to deal with that year was the onset of bowel incontinence. I had uncontrollable diarrhoea and, because I had no sensation below my waist, I was unable to control it and consequently regularly had accidents. The most difficult aspect of this was that when I started to eat a meal the food would exit minutes after I swallowed it. This caused me immense problems eating out at a restaurant. I knew before I started eating that I would have an accident almost immediately and would have to make my way to the toilet to try to clean myself up. Strangely enough it was nothing like as distressing as I had assumed it would be. I was still habitually wearing my "incontinence survival outfit", because I was still having problems with bladder control, which meant that nobody else knew that I had had an accident. I developed the strategy of always carrying spare clean underwear in my handbag and a plastic bag to put the soiled ones in. It became nothing more than another, less than desirable, fact of MS life.

I had never mentioned the bowel incontinence either to Ray or Dr O'Connor. In reading all the MS self-help books I had never seen it mentioned other than in the context of constipation, which is the most usual bowel effect of MS. Consequently the whole subject was largely taboo as far as I was concerned. I think that it is not mentioned for two reasons. Firstly, as I said, it is not a common MS symptom, and secondly because there is very little that can be done about it. With bladder incontinence there are several drugs that can be used to help and ultimately self-catheterisation is a solution. With bowel incontinence there seem to be no drugs that are used to control it and, other than using incontinence pads, there is little that can be done, or so I then thought.

Finally it had got past a joke and so, when seeing Dr O'Connor one day when he asked, as he habitually did, how my "waterworks" were, I told him about the bladder incontinence. He immediately said with a huge grin, "Oh! that's easy . . . we will get you self-catheterising." I replied that I did not wish to do that. He looked surprised and said, "But if you do that you can be safe for several hours!" I repeated that I had no intention of self-catheterising. By then he was looking rather confused and asked me why I didn't want to do it. I told him that I had known other people who had done it and frankly I was not prepared to put myself through that. He then blustered a bit and said, "At least let me set up an appointment with the incontinence adviser for you!" I once again refused his offer. Again he asked me why not and I explained to him that all it would achieve was to waste both their and my time as they would only try and convince me to self-catheterise. He sighed in resignation and scribbled a note in my file. It probably said something along the lines of "Cari is a non-compliant patient"! I then took a deep breath and said, "If you really want to do something to help then you can sort out the bowel incontinence for me." He looked perturbed and perhaps a little embarrassed and asked me how much of a problem it was and how I was coping with it. I told him how it was affecting me and that basically I went home several times a day to clean myself up and change my clothes before returning to the office. Although he said in a concerned voice, "We really must get that sorted out for you", he made no suggestions then as to how he was going to do it.

The next day I went to see Ray whom I normally saw once a week at his request. I told him about my meeting with Dr O'Connor and, therefore, told him for the first time about the bowel incontinence. He observed that it was in effect the same as spastic colon (irritable bowel syndrome – IBS), although caused by the colon being paralysed by the MS, and thought it would be worth trying me on Colofac, a drug used to treat IBS. He instructed me to take one tablet half an hour before I had a meal and to let him know if it helped. Actually it helped enormously almost immediately. It amused me that it took an ordinary GP to sort me out when the neurologists had not yet come up with any suggestions as to what to do.

However, despite the drugs helping, I still had accidents on occasion. Believe it or not one of the things that happened to me during the MS years that makes me laugh the most involved bowel incontinence. It was one of those events that should never have happened. It was the day that the clocks went back. I had changed all the clocks in my flat but had forgotten to alter my watch. I had just had breakfast and decided I would go out to Safeway to get some things that I needed. I reached the shop, which was only a few hundred yards from my flat, to discover it was still closed. It transpired, of course, that I was an hour early but had not realised it because I had not changed the time on my watch. I turned around to make my way home again and was about half-way up the street when I realised I desperately needed to go to the toilet. I tried my best to get home as quickly as possible and finally made it back to the block of flats. The situation was getting more desperate by the minute but I made it back to my flat and walked through the door in jubilation at having made it back in time. I got to the bathroom feeling very pleased with myself and went to unzip my jeans. The zip jammed! I tugged at the zip assuming it would move, but no, it was well and truly stuck. As I was standing there, only inches away from the toilet, losing more control of my bowels by the minute, I got the giggles. It struck me as so ironic that I couldn't help but laugh. I finally went and got a Stanley knife from the kitchen and cut the zip out of my jeans, by which time, of course, it was too late. Not only had I had a childish accident but I had ruined a perfectly good pair of jeans and all I could do was giggle helplessly. I think part of what made me laugh was that, even while it was happening, I could hear the story in my head as I would later tell it.

The other big taboo with the doctors, as far as women with MS are concerned, is female sexual dysfunction. Once again, the self-help books all talked about male sexual dysfunction and what can be done about it, but there was never any mention of the problems women with MS have with regard to sex. I think that the male medics assume that women can still be made love to whether they can feel it or not, so it doesn't really matter. I used to joke that the neurologists were terrified of anything "below the knicker line". If it was an issue of incontinence then they immediately brought in the incontinence adviser. Sex was never mentioned. They would do pin-prick tests all over my body to see if there was any loss of sensation, but they avoided the knicker area like it was a minefield. I am sure that doctors become neurologists because they don't have to deal with anything embarrassing to them. There were several problems that I encountered when it came to sex during that year. The most obvious was that I was numb from mid-chest down and, therefore, could feel absolutely nothing when making love.

Frankly it felt like being abused. The second was that I would get agonising cramp in my thigh muscles. It's all very well thrashing around and groaning when making love but not if your lover thinks you are enjoying yourself when really you are in pain from cramp in your legs! There I was shouting "No no . . . please . . . no" and he assumed I was in ecstasy! I could not remember when I had last felt aroused, let alone been able to have an orgasm.

It finally reached the stage where I could not bear the thought of being made love to any more. I was terrified to tell my lover as I was sure he would think that I was no longer worth bothering with. Actually I was amazed that he had stuck with me through the MS that far. Anyway, one evening things were progressing towards the inevitable and I knew I had to say something. I steeled myself and said, "Look, making love is really difficult for me now, sweetheart. I can't feel anything and it just serves to remind me that things are very wrong with my body." There, I had said it; I braced myself for the expected rejection. The way he reacted amazed me. He lay back on the bed, put his hands behind his head and, with a grin, said, "OK. There's nothing wrong with your mouth is there? And at least it will keep you quiet for a while!" He had said the perfect thing. He was telling me, in not so many words, that I was no different to him than the way I had been before MS hit. Different was different, not less. I think I loved him more at that moment than I ever had before.

Actually, I think it was easier for me to cope with MS than it was for my family and friends on the whole, although they all did their best. My sister, Viki, coped by trying to be over-protective towards me, something she was doomed to fail in. I have never reacted well to people trying to look after me or protect me. My brother, Clive was understandably upset but, having had an appalling accident the year before where he badly sliced the fingers of his right hand with a circular saw, leaving him with one missing and one inoperative, he understood far more about what I was dealing with in terms of major changes in life than anyone else in my family. Hilary, my sister-in-law, was pure magic. She alternated between emotionally supporting me, cheering me up by teasing me about whether I could beat my youngest niece, Alice, to her feet or getting control of her bodily functions, and on many occasions providing me with good advice on how to cope with certain situations. My father tried his hardest but my diagnosis must have devastated him. Not long after I had been diagnosed I remember him almost screaming down the phone, "You broke my fucking heart when you got MS." I know he was incredibly upset but for a while I felt as if he was blaming me, that somehow he was accusing me of getting MS on purpose. My mother bore the brunt of my endless phone calls. I needed to talk and talk and talk. I was telling the story of what had happened to me almost obsessively. It must have been enormously hard on her just to listen when she must have felt so helpless in terms of being able to do anything for her youngest child. My quarterly phone bill was enormous during the MS years!

I felt constantly during that time that I had to be strong to protect the people I cared for. I could not cope with them being upset as well as me. It was hard to feel, as indeed I always had, that my role in life was to be the strong one, the coper, the one who carries other people's pain rather than offload my own. My distress was always that I knew nobody strong enough to hear my darkest thoughts and bear them alongside me.

My first MS treatment breakthrough occurred in September 1993. I had already had two courses of intravenous steroids, once in December 1992 and again in July 1993. By the end of

September 1993 I was in a pretty bad physical state. My legs would barely hold me even with using crutches. The bladder and bowel incontinence were out of control. I had constant optic neuritis which made my sight foggy, and the fatigue was overwhelming. Dr O'Connor showed his true colours in a consultation that month. He had just run through the regular tests of strength, balance, sensation and sight when, for the first time, he took my pulse and blood pressure. He then walked back to his desk and said, "You are very fit you know!" I grinned wryly at the irony of his statement and said, "Oh sure. I have an incurable disabling disease and you say I am very fit." He then chuckled, leaned back in his chair, put his hands behind his head, grinned and said, "Oh, MS doesn't make you ill . . . it just paralyses you." I thought that his response was terribly funny but when I repeated it to my family they were horrified at how insensitive his remark was. I failed miserably in trying to explain to them why I found his remark so amusing. I liked his attitude and the fact that he didn't try and hide the truth of my illness from me. The last thing in the world Dr O'Connor would ever have done was to patronise me.

Dr O'Connor was more than a little worried about the rate at which I was deteriorating but he knew he couldn't give me another course of steroids so soon after the last one. He pondered the situation for a while and then said, "Look. I can't give you another five-day course of Methyl Prednisolone but how about I give you a one-day dose?" I knew he was offering it as a consolation prize but right then I was ready to agree to anything. I was clutching at straws. He arranged for me to go to the ward the next day for an intravenous drip and I turned up. Dean was still my SHO so I was happy about having to go in. He wasn't surprised to hear that I was only having a one-off dose of steroids as Dr O'Connor had briefed him the evening before. He put the Venflon in without a problem and left me to regulate the speed of the drip as he trusted me to know how it should be done. An hour later I walked out of the hospital feeling decidedly less wobbly. The next morning I discovered that I was able to walk down the corridor in my block of flats without my crutches! I was amazed that a single dose had such a dramatic effect. A week later the effect wore off and I was back to square one again. I went back to see Dr O'Connor who, by then, had told his secretary that if I rang up I could see him the same day. I told him what had happened after the steroids and he was amazed. He said that he had never heard of a response like mine before, that I must be incredibly sensitive to steroids. He then decided to try the same dose again to see what would happen. Again I observed the same effect but this time it lasted only twenty-four hours and I was back in trouble again.

I went back to see Dr O'Connor to report the effect. He pondered the phenomenon for a moment and then said, "I haven't the faintest idea what is going on here. Look. Your hunches have been good so far. What do you want to do?" By then I had begun to think that since I responded so well to steroids and relapsed so fast afterwards, that maybe I was rebounding from the high doses that they habitually used and that it looked as if the one-day dose was still too high for me. I explained this to Dr O'Connor and he said, "OK. So what do you suggest?" I told him I wanted a single 250 mg dose instead of the previous 500 mg to see what would happen and he happily agreed to give it a go.

On 20 October Dr O'Connor wrote to Ray reporting on what we were doing. He wrote:

I saw Cari in my follow-up clinic today and there is no

doubt that she does respond to a single intravenous dose of prednisolone. Unfortunately, however, the response does not last very long. Nevertheless, although she remains very unsteady, I think the power in her legs has improved and we plan to give her a futher intravenous infusion towards the end of the week. We are going to try her on 250 mg instead of 500 mg.

I had the IV drip on Friday afternoon and when lying in bed that night I realised that the MS attack had been aborted. It wasn't that my symptoms went away because they hadn't. It was a physical sensation or knowledge that the MS wasn't active. I found it impossible to explain to anyone how it felt, but I *knew* the attack had aborted. I remained physically stable for nearly two weeks and then things started to deteriorate again. I saw Dr O'Connor and explained exactly what had happened. He was very pleased and immediately set it up for me to have another dose. He said that I could have steroids at that level every two weeks for a while to see what happened. We did this several times but it was obvious that the effect only lasted just under two weeks.

By 17 December I was able to do away with my crutches and Dr O'Connor wrote to Ray saying:

She is now able to walk without any aids and, apart from some ataxia of gait, is really doing very well. So far the experiment seems to be working quite well but I think it is too early as yet to tell whether it will keep her free of further attacks.

For the first time since it hit, I had some way of controlling the MS. Dr O'Connor had explained to me that although he was happy for me to have steroids every two weeks, sooner or later they would fail to work as my body got used to them. I decided there and then that the day the steroids failed I would kill myself. I believed that there was no way I would ever come up with another idea for controlling the MS. I knew that if I lost control of the MS again and had no way back I was simply not prepared to stick around and see what happened.

As the months progressed and my symptoms became more stable I began to notice a pattern emerging of when I needed the steroids. It appeared that I really only needed them every four weeks. It was just before Christmas 1993 and I realised that I was due to have a period over the Christmas week. This would not have mattered if it were not for the fact that every time I had a period I got a migraine, and I didn't really fancy having a migraine at Christmas. I decided that I would take the contraceptive pill without a break and so avoid a period and, therefore, a migraine. What amazed me was that despite late nights, combined with too much drink and excitement, the MS didn't deteriorate any further. I went back to the hospital the day I got back from Christmas at Clive's and told them that I really didn't need the steroids. But I had the drip anyway. On my thirty-fourth birthday, on 7 January, I drank some cheap champagne and promptly developed a migraine. Within half an hour my legs started to get weak and spastic. My obsessive little researcher's brain started to click over. I began to think over the pattern of Christmas not having a migraine and then my reaction to having a migraine on my birthday and began to realise that maybe it was monthly migraines that were flipping the MS out. I went to see Dr O'Connor and put my theory to him. He brushed it off saying, "Rubbish. One is neurological and one is vascular. There is no way there can be any connection." I then looked at him and said, "Hang on. You have told me that my hunches have been good, so humour me." He nodded at me and said, "OK. Go on then." I explained to him what my theory was and he said, 'So you are not saying that the migraines cause the MS symptoms?" I shook my head and replied, "Of course not!" Then he said "So you are saying that the migraines cause the MS to flare up?" I nodded and said "Yup. Sure am." He then grinned and said, "Oh well. That is perfectly likely." "At last!" I thought.

I decided that I would take the contraceptive pill without having a break each month and, thereby, prevent monthly migraines. I went and asked Ray if that would be OK and he was perfectly amenable to my doing it. I continued to do that and realised very quickly that I could stretch the gap between the steroids much longer than two weeks. I actually managed to last for six weeks without them on one occasion. Unfortunately I kept getting viruses or bugs and that always flipped the MS out again. So it was back to steroids every two weeks for a while. I really did think that I had got the MS sussed. OK, so I still had a lot of symptoms but I had succeeded in stopping the relentless downhill slide. The longer I kept the MS at bay the more I was regaining both my physical and psychological strength. All in all I was feeling much more positive about life. This regime kept me going until July 1994. It was then that the true horror story began.

✦

CHAPTER FOUR

Going Under

✦

Here I was in July 1994 having fought tooth and nail with every ounce of energy I had since October 1992. I had worked out how to use the steroids to keep the MS at least partially under control. I had worked out that monthly migraines were causing monthly MS attacks and had sorted *that* out. I really thought that I had got a handle on the beast. And then, out of the blue, another big MS attack blew sky high.

I was sitting in the waiting room at the hospital waiting for my appointment with Dr O'Connor. As usual he was running about an hour late so I had quite a long time to sit around twiddling my thumbs. I had arrived at the hospital walking quite well and not feeling too bad at all. Dr O'Connor finally came out of his office and called out to me. I went to stand up and realised with horror that my legs had given out on me. I had a great deal of trouble walking to his office as my knees get snapping out under me. Dr O'Connor watched me walk towards him and said, "What on earth has happened?" I explained to him that the MS seemed to have gone into freefall during the past hour as I was sitting waiting for him. That day he had a medical visitor with him to observe the consultation. He got me up on the examination couch and checked out the strength and coordination in my legs and commented that the deterioration was dramatic. He then started to check my eyes and gave the impression of having found something unusual. He called the visitor over and said to her, "Take a look at this. She has got a right intranuclear. We don't often see that." They spent some time taking it in turns to look at my eyes and getting me to follow their finger from one side to the other. They seemed inappropriately excited by it! I had no idea what an optic intranuclear was so I asked Dr O'Connor to explain what he found so interesting. It transpired that my right eye was not tracking at the same speed as my left one. It must have looked weird! He finally finished checking me out and said, "What do you think. Time for steroids?" I agreed whole-heartedly and thought that would sort me out as it had on the previous occasions. As he was so concerned about me he arranged for me to have the steroids before I left the hospital but told me to come back and see him in two weeks' time.

But despite the steroids I was once again chronically fatigued, losing my balance and my legs were weak and ataxic (uncoordinated) and I was, therefore, once again having a lot of trouble walking. I could not believe that I had lost it all again. I was shocked beyond belief by the realisation that the MS was still out of control despite the regular doses of steroids and all the work I had put into it. For the first time the steroids didn't work their magic on me. What scared me the most was the fear that the steroids had finally failed, in which case there was nothing else left to try. There had always been the possibility that having the steroids too often would lead to them becoming ineffective in terms of holding the MS. I had said, right from the start, that the time that the steroids failed I would end it, I would pull the plug, I would kill myself. Well, here it was as far as I was concerned. The end of the line.

I went back to see Dr O'Connor a week later at his Tuesday clinic and told him that the steroids had had no effect. He checked me out again and concurred that I was no better and, therefore, there was no use in giving me more steroids at the moment. As I was leaving his office he called out after me, "Come back and see me on Friday." He had never seen me twice in one week no matter how bad I had been, so I was more than a little surprised. I continued to deteriorate physically and consequently started to slide into depression. It felt as if all that fighting had been for nothing and I was emotionally exhausted. I had completely run out of the strength to fight again, and anyway, I reckoned that I had worked out everything that I possibly could. There was nothing left to try. There was no longer, as far as I was concerned, any hope. Dr O'Connor saw me at his Friday clinic that week, and again saw no improvement and once again said, "Come back next Tuesday to see me." By then I was getting worried. I began to think that there was something he wasn't telling me. Why on earth would he want to keep seeing me twice a week unless he had found something that truly worried him? I talked it over with a couple of friends and they agreed with my logic. I went back to see him the next Tuesday and he again checked me out. As I was sitting on the examination couch and he had finished doing the tests I said to him, "Listen. It's not a problem but why are you seeing me so often at the moment?" He replied, "Well you only live just round the corner don't you?" I repeated that it wasn't a problem but I was beginning to wonder why he wanted to see me at every clinic. He acted as if he was embarrassed and finally said "I felt bad about the fact that the steroids failed and that I can't do anything more for you at the moment. I just didn't want you to feel that I had abandoned you." I could have hugged him. I didn't expect my consultant neurologist actually to care about me to that extent.

On the evening of 20 July I was sitting at home and was feeling so scared and miserable that I just *had* to have someone to talk to. I knew someone, Chris, who I had met on the MS news group on the computer Internet and we had become good friends by phoning each other every week although we had never met. As he also had MS I guessed he would understand what I was talking about and how I was feeling. That was something that was vitally important. There was little point in talking to someone who didn't have MS as, no matter how sympathetic they were, they simply would not be able to relate to what I was talking about. I rang him and, thankfully he was there. "Hello" he said. I managed to say "Chris, it's Cari" before my voice broke. For the next five or six minutes I couldn't talk as I had started crying and I knew that if I said anything I would completely lose control. "What's happened, Cari? What's wrong?" Chris said. I began to talk through the tears and told him that I felt I had reached the end of the line, and that I couldn't go on any longer. That I was exhausted from the relentless battle against MS. He talked me through it as best he could, reminding me that I had been there before and that I had come through it, and that I would again. For all the impact it was having on me he could have been talking to a brick wall. The more he tried to boost me up the more distressed I became. I didn't *want* to fight any more. I truly wanted to give up. Chris talked to me until midnight by which time he had me laughing through my tears. I don't quite know what I would have done without him that night. He finally said to me, "You're OK Cari. You can hack it", to which I replied wearily, "Yeah. Unfortunately you are probably right." We said goodnight and I lay down in bed and turned the light off.

I was lying there thinking, "It's OK kiddo. Come on. You can do it. Just sleep the pain away like you have before," when, suddenly, I found myself doing something I hadn't done since I was a young teenager. I wasn't exactly praying, it was more like plea bargaining! I caught myself thinking, "OK God. Just give me one little positive sign that you are on my side and I will come over to yours." At that moment I became aware of the sound of running water. I listened for a moment and assumed it was just a tap running in the flat next door. I went back to what I had been thinking "Just let me know you are on my side OK?" Again I became aware of the sound of running water and decided I wouldn't be able to settle unless I went to the bathroom and made sure I hadn't left a tap running. I got up and staggered to the bathroom, switched on the light and was greeted by the sight of my bathroom floor awash and a veritable Niagara Falls coming from the base of the toilet cistern. I stood there for a second thinking, "What the hell!" and then galvanised into action. I flushed the toilet, assuming that the ballcock had jammed and the water was coming out of the overflow. The torrent of water got even worse so I flushed it again. No luck. I had grabbed a container from the kitchen and started to catch the water and bail out as fast as I could. I threw all the towels I had on the floor to sop up some of the water which by then I was paddling in. I couldn't catch the water and empty the container as fast as it was flowing and I couldn't get a big enough bucket under it due to the positioning of the toilet close to the wall. I knew I had to get downstairs to the night porter to get him to call a plumber or something but was faced with the dilemma of leaving the bathroom to flood in the meantime. I finally turned my back on the flood and made my way down the stairs on badly shaking legs.

The porter came up to my flat with me and realised that there was a large crack in the base of the cistern. He said that we had to drain the cistern and find a way of preventing it from filling up again until he could get the plumber to come first thing in the morning to replace the cistern. After a few abortive efforts we finally came up with the novel idea of using my hairbrush to prop up the arm of the ballcock to prevent the cistern from filling again. He left saying that the plumber would turn up at six o'clock in the morning. I spent the next half an hour sitting on the edge of the bath, catching the water in a bowl, as the cistern emptied. Finally the water stopped and I picked up the towels, threw them in the bath and cleared up as best I could. I gave the precarious hairbrush mechanism one last doubtful look, turned the light off and went back to my bedroom.

Totally exhausted, I sat down on the floor and wondered when on earth this hell was going to come to an end. As I sat there I suddenly remembered what I had been thinking seconds before the toilet debacle. I had been plea bargaining with God. It pulled me up short and I thought, "You bastard! All I asked for was one little positive sign and *this* is your response!" At that moment I had no doubt at all that God existed but that he was an evil bugger. I said out loud, "OK. I get the message. I offered to come over to your side and you have told me to go to hell. Fine." By now it was half past one in the morning but I needed to talk to someone to tell them about what had just happened with my flood. It would have been unreasonable to ring Chris again as he had MS and sleep is vital to all of us who are afflicted. I wanted to phone Hilary but, as a mother of four children, it would have been unfair to her. I remembered that the MS Society had a twenty-four hour counselling line but, try as I might, I could not find the piece of paper with the number on it. In desperation I rang Directory Enquiries but they were unable to find any listing for the MS counselling line. They seemed to realise that I was desperate as they kept on and on trying to find a number for me. They finally said, "I have the number for the central London Samaritans if you would like that." I replied that I thought it might not be a bad idea and wrote the number down.

Could I really summon up the courage to ring the Samaritans? After all, I wasn't seriously suicidal and, as far as I was concerned, that is all the Samaritans were there for. Finally my desperate need to talk to someone overrode my misgivings and I picked up the phone and dialled. I was amazed when the phone was answered immediately. "Hello. Samaritans. How can I help you?" a soft, gentle voice said. I gulped and said, "Umm . . . well . . . I'm not suicidal or anything but I wondered if I could just talk to someone for a moment?" "Of course you can," he replied, "Would you like to talk to me?" "Yes please" I said. There was a pause and then he asked "What's been happening?" I started to tell him about the toilet cistern bursting and the resultant flood and was largely laughing it off. "I know it's a pretty stupid thing to get upset about," I heard myself say. He replied "No. It's not stupid and, anyway, things are harder to deal with in the early hours of the morning aren't they?" I talked a little more about it and then found myself saying something I had had no intention of doing "And to cap it all," I said, "I've got MS." He paused again and then said, "That must be very hard for you." His voice was so gentle and cuddly that his sympathy began to break my control. "How long have you had it?" he asked. I explained what had happened in November 1992 and the fact that I was in the middle of another attack and that the steroids had failed. He made soothing, understanding noises as I talked and, when I finally stopped, he said sadly, "Life isn't being fair to you is it?" That was it. I sobbed "No . . . I can't take any more. I've had enough."

Once I had started to cry there was no way I could stop. I must have cried for at least five minutes without him saying anything. As I began to calm down a bit I said, "I'm sorry. I didn't mean to do that." "That's OK," he said. "You have a right to cry." That nearly broke me again but I tried hard not to lose control. He then said "My name's Simon . . . what's yours?" "Cari," I sobbed. He commented on the fact that it was an unusual name and then said "Have you thought about suicide, Cari?" Having started out by saying that I wasn't suicidal I had to admit that, yes, I was considering suicide. "Have you thought about how you would do it?" he asked. I told him that I had a stockpile of painkillers and knew that there were enough to do the trick. "The thing is," I said, "I am terrified of getting so ill that I'm institutionalised and then I won't be allowed to kill myself. So I want to do it before I gets that bad." Simon told me that it was incredibly important that I keep that control and that I must always know I have the choice to kill myself if I wanted to. "Do you feel that you want to kill yourself now?" he asked. I was forced to admit that indeed I did. "Where are you in London, Cari?" he asked. "Just round the corner from the British Museum," I responded.

By this time I had been talking to him for nearly an hour and a half and was feeling very tired, so the full, possible, implication of his question didn't hit me. He then said "We are not far from you . . . would you come and see me tomorrow and have a coffee and a chat?" "I don't know" I replied. "Well, would you like me to come and see you?" he then asked. "Do you do that?" I asked him, "I thought the Samaritans only worked over the phone." He explained that they have a drop-in centre which is open all day, every day, and that I could turn up whenever I wanted. I began to think that maybe he was tracing the call and that someone would turn up on my doorstep any minute. But he had finally managed to calm me down so I said "Listen, Thanks for everything. I think I'm OK now". "That's all right," he said. "You know we are always here. Ring whenever you want to." I thanked Simon again and put the phone down feeling completely drained. It was now two o'clock in the morning and the plumber was due to turn up in four hours time. I had been crying, on and off, for nearly four hours and felt terrible. My head ached, my eyes were sore and I had been chain-smoking most of the time. I went to check on the hairbrush system one last time and then crawled into bed. My mind whirled with thoughts and feelings and sleep would not come.

I have often thought that if Simon had tried to talk me out of killing myself I wouldn't have listened. The fact that he legitimised the way I was feeling and that he said it was OK to want to commit suicide took the pressure off having to do it that night. I truly believe that without having made contact with Simon then I would have gone ahead and killed myself after the flood. Since I discovered my treatment I have often wanted to ring Simon the Samaritan and say "Heh. Have you *any* idea what *wouldn't* have happened if I hadn't talked to you that night?"

After I had been lying awake in bed for a while I put the radio on and lay listening to it until I saw the dawn break, at which point I got up and made ready for the plumber's arrival. Promptly at six o'clock there was a knock on the front door. I opened it to the plumber and explained to him the flood of the previous night. He looked into the cistern and said, "I see. There is a big crack there. You will have to have a new cistern." He wasn't sure whether he would be able to get a cistern that fitted the unit as it was quite old and, as a consequence, I might have to have a brand new unit. He told me that he would go away and try to track down a new cistern and would come back at one o'clock and that I should have the cash waiting for him as he wouldn't take a cheque.

As luck would have it, I had an appointment with Steve, my counsellor, at ten o'clock that morning so, after the plumber had gone, I got myself ready and left the flat. I was glad to be seeing Steve as I especially needed support that day. I arrived and, after a few minutes' wait, he came out of his office to get me. He started the session as usual by saying, "Tell me about what has been happening in the past week." I responded by telling him what had happened the night before. Predictably I got upset and started crying again. As I was so distressed I can't fully remember the conversation but somehow we got onto talking about the fact that I was always hoping to find someone who was strong enough to support me. We were discussing how important Dean had been to me in terms of being able to see through my bluster and bluff to the pain inside when, suddenly, Steve said, "Only a psychopath could deal with you." I looked up, expecting him to follow up his statement by saying, "Is that what you think?" but when I asked, "What do you mean?" he replied, "Only someone without a heart or brain could cope with you." Before I could respond he opened his diary and said, "Same time next week?" I promptly forgot what he had said as I was preoccupied with the problem of getting to the bank and taking out the cash I needed for the plumber who was due to turn up at my flat in less than an hour. I got to the bank, took out the money I needed and made my way back to my flat. When the plumber turned up I was relieved to see that he had managed to find a matching cistern which he rapidly fitted. I paid him and he went on his way.

As it was only lunchtime I decided to go to the office. I arrived and, after having told my Niagara Falls toilet story to a few people, settled down in front on my computer to do some work. As I was sitting there typing a letter I suddenly remembered what Steve had said at the end of the session that morning. "What the hell did he mean? Why on earth did he say that?" I thought. I pondered it for a while, getting more upset and angry by the minute. I started getting very confused as I began to think that he must have been telling me that *he* couldn't cope with me any longer. If he was telling me that only a psychopath could deal with me then either he was saying that *he* was a psychopath (which I assumed was not the case) or he was letting me know that he couldn't cope with me. I became increasingly upset as the afternoon wore on. What could I do? For the past year I would have turned to Steve to discuss it. Who could I turn to now that he had betrayed me? Finally I went home but the thoughts kept running around inside my head. Why had he betrayed me? Why had he abandoned me when I needed him the most? What had I done wrong? I decided to ring the MS counselling line for the first time (I had found the number by then). I rang the number and, after fifteen minutes of the line being engaged, I got through to Ann, the lady who was taking calls on that day. All the people who manned the counselling line had MS themselves so they were probably the perfect people for me to talk to right then.

I told Ann that I had a problem with my counsellor and explained to her what had happened that morning with Steve. "He said *what*?!" she shrieked down the phone. "Yup" I replied "He said that only a psychopath could deal with me." "Sack him," said Ann, "Report him to his professional body." Ann was incensed that any counsellor could do that to a client. I explained to her that I was very confused about why he had done it and asked her if she could offer any suggestions. "It is perfectly obvious to me, Cari," she replied, "He almost certainly feels that you are more competent than him in terms of dealing with the MS and your reactions to it and you make him feel inadequate." She then went on to say that I was better off without him. She then asked me about my history of MS, so I told her my story of diagnosis and how the disease had progressed during the previous twenty-one months. Suddenly she said, "Look. We are told never to reveal anything about ourselves when we are dealing with people on the counselling line, but I have to tell you my story." I laughed and promised not to tell on her. Ann then explained to me that she had encountered a very similar experience as me in terms of not being told what the diagnosis was. We bitched for a while about medics who tell lies and generally had a mutual rage session about doctors. We finally said goodbye and I put the phone down feeling much better about the Steve situation.

I thought long and hard over the next week about what I was going to do about Steve. I decided that when I next saw him I would demand an answer to why he had said what he did. He owed me that much at least. A week after the momentous session I went back to see him as arranged. I had carefully planned how I intended to play the session. This time I was not sitting in the chair in the corridor waiting for him when he came to get me. I stood outside his office door. As it was sunny that day I was wearing sunglasses and I had decided to keep them on during the session so he couldn't see my eyes. I was damned if I would ever let him see me get upset again. The balance of power was going to change radically in that session. Steve greeted me as he always had, as if nothing had happened. I walked into his office and he said, as he always did, "Have a seat." "Not yet," I said and stood there looking at him. "Before you say anything else," I said, "I want to know why you said that only a psychopath could deal with me." He started to say, "Well you were feeling . . ." when I interrupted and said, "I know perfectly well how I was feeling and I am not interested in what you have to say about that. I want an answer, Steve."

It must have been obvious that I was extremely angry with him. "OK," he said, "Have a seat and we'll talk about it". I grudgingly sat down and stared at him. "We were talking about Dean and how he saw through your bluff to the pain beneath," he began. "Correct," I snapped. "And I was reflecting back to you that you had unrealistic expectations of other people," he continued. "Bullshit," I retorted. "Well I think you do expect too much of other people, Cari" he said, "You are much stronger than them." I brushed that off and said, "So you thought that telling someone who had been up all night and who was extremely distressed that only a psychopath could deal with them was helpful did you?" He tried to steer the conversation in different directions, made excuses by trying to make it my responsibility and generally avoided the issue. I kept trying to get him to give me an answer and got absolutely nowhere. Every time I threw the question at him he avoided the issue. I delivered the final blow when, near the end of the hour when he normally would say, "We must end now", I looked at my watch and said "Right. Time is up, I have to go now", and got to my feet. "Shall we meet at the same time next week?" he asked. I looked at him and said, "I am not sure whether I ever want to see you again, Steve." That took him by surprise. For the first time in that session he seemed to be genuinely rattled. "Well, can I pencil you in for next week anyway?" he asked me. "No," I replied. I didn't tell him that I would be away then and couldn't go anyway. "Oh," he said sounding somewhat perturbed. "Well, what about the week after then? You don't have to turn up if you don't want to" he offered. "Alright" I said "But don't hold your breath. I probably won't come. I'm not sure if I can ever trust you again." I started to walk out of his office and he said the same thing as he always had, "Take care then." I turned round to face him and said, "Don't you think it is a little late for that?" and left.

As it happened, I had an appointment with Ray immediately after seeing Steve. I went into Ray's office and sat down in silence. He smiled at me and said, "How are things this week?" I immediately told him about what had happened with Steve and asked, "Do you think he should have said that? Is there any excuse?" Ray looked at me and shook his head. "No," he said "Do you want me to try and find a new counsellor for you?" I replied that it might not be a bad idea. Ray told me that he would sort someone out for me but he would have to make sure it was the right person this time. I reminded him that for the best part of a year Steve had been perfect for me. He had been my anchor in the midst of the storm, my safe place once a week. But, for whatever reason, the relationship had broken down now.

Ray reassured me that it wasn't my fault and that sometimes these things happen after a long-term relationship with a counsellor, that essentially counsellor and client get to know each other too well. I left feeling much better about the situation with Steve. At the very least I had stood up to him and let him know how I felt.

That afternoon I rang Hilary, my sister-in-law, to tell her about my flood in the early hours of the morning. I told her about my plea-bargaining with God and what the response I got was. To me it was a very funny story but, as she and Clive are both Christians, I mentioned that I hoped I wasn't offending her by saying that I thought God was an absolute bastard. Hilary laughed and said "I think God is big enough to cope with that, Cari". "Whatever," I replied "but you have to admit it was a pretty evil response." She laughed again and said "He knows you too well. If something had gone right the next day you would simply have assumed it was a lucky occurrence. You have to admit that his immediate response made you sit up and take notice." She was right, of course, but I didn't like the idea that there was a power out there who knew me that well!

The reason I had told Steve that I could not see him the following week was because Viki, my sister, had invited me to go and stay with her for a few days. The next day I packed a bag and caught the train to Portsmouth. I had mixed feelings about going away. When I was in an MS attack I didn't want to be too far away from home and, therefore, from Ray and Dr O'Connor in case something went wrong. Viki had asked me on several occasions to go and stay with her and had been so insistent this time that I needed a holiday that I had felt bad about turning her down yet again. She had told me that she would take the week off work and we would have a nice time together. Her husband

Andy met me at the station and drove me back to their cottage. We had a pleasant dinner that evening (Viki is an exceptionally accomplished cook) and I went to bed feeling quite relaxed. The next day Viki told me that she had to go into work later that morning but would be home by mid-afternoon. I was somewhat disappointed but we went to the stables to see her horse before she left for work. For the rest of the day I was left on my own with only the two cats, Hector and Tygar, for company. I spent the day watching television and smoking and cuddling the cats, when they would let me. Viki finally came back at about half past four and immediately asked me if I wanted to go shopping. I wasn't too thrilled at the idea as my walking was less than good but I agreed to go anyway.

This pattern was repeated over the next two days. I was feeling increasingly alienated and depressed as I was removed from my normal support system of friends and the general routine of my life. I distracted myself by watching the afternoon "soaps" on television. At least while I was lost in the trivia of the stories I could forget about MS for a while. I was mindlessly watching a programme when the commercial break came on. Suddenly the MS Society advertisement started. There it was, slamming the reality of the disease in my face again. I sat there watching the image of a perfect, young female body being held up by her equally perfect partner. The words echoed through my brain, "Who will be there to pick up the pieces if MS hits?" I started to choke up and, when the MS Society byline "The MS Society. A Hope in Hell" was flashed up, I broke down into tears. I *hated* that advertising campaign. I still do for that matter. Who on earth did they think they were to say that just because I had been diagnosed with MS that my life was hell? Hadn't they ever considered what effect that would have on people who were newly diagnosed and on their friends and families? Was there no way to escape MS? I felt as if I couldn't live for a second without someone or something reminding me about it. But then I fell back on my old coping strategy of getting angry. I have always preferred to be angry rather than upset. It goes some way to making me feel stronger. My anger must have shown because the cats wouldn't come near me!

Viki came home later that afternoon and, as the weather was nice, decided that we would have dinner outside that night. At about eight o'clock we sat down to dinner. Viki and Andy had only been married for two and a half years so he didn't know me very well and we hadn't spoken in depth on many occasions. He started asking me about the MS and how I had been coping with it. He was genuinely interested and wanted to understand. Viki had been contributing to the conversation but I had found it annoying when she followed up what I said by saying things like "But it wasn't that bad really" or "But you coped well." She then said, "I don't see why you can't just come to terms with it." I felt very frustrated as I couldn't make her understand how impossible it was for me to come to terms with having my normal life and future taken away at the age of thirty-one. After half an hour or so Viki suddenly piped up, rather aggressively, "If I got MS I would just get on with my life and not let it affect me." I couldn't believe what I was hearing. I assume it was yet another example of denial. I had discovered that the knowledge that MS can hit anyone out of the blue scared some people to death. It made them face their own mortality. I guess Viki was only doing the same. At that time when I was so depressed and emotionally exhausted the last thing I needed was for someone to, in effect, tell me that I should be coping better and that I was being a failure. I tried to explain to her that it wasn't that simple and that MS doesn't allow you to ignore it. By this time I was crying and had pretty much given up on making anyone understand what I was going through. Viki finally realised that I was upset and tried to make amends. But the damage had been done.

At the end of the week I returned to London. I was determined that this time I was going to go ahead and kill myself and that nothing was going to stop me. I refused to fight for a future that I had no desire to stick around for. A few days after returning home I was sitting on the floor in my flat one evening with my stockpile of painkillers spread out on the floor in front of me. I knew that there were enough to do the trick. Even if they didn't kill me outright they would put me in a coma and, as no one could get into my flat once the door was bolted from the inside, I would die in due course. I started to think about the people I would be leaving behind and came to the conclusion that they would be better off without me. Then my thoughts turned to Ray. He had been unequivocally supportive to me since I became his patient and I felt that I owed it to him to not kill myself until I had given him the chance to try everything he could for me. In this case that meant putting me onto anti-depressants. The next day I went to see Ray and told him that I wanted to be put onto anti-depressants as I was suicidally depressed. He told me that he was relieved as he had thought for some time that I would benefit from them. I sighed and said, "I just want a holiday from the MS." "I know," he said sadly. "I'm sorry that I can't do that for you. At least anti-depressants will give you a holiday from the way you feel at the moment." He wrote me a prescription and told me to take one tablet at night before I went to bed as they would make me drowsy. He then told me that he would be away on holiday for three weeks from the next day onward but that he would brief one of his colleagues, Michael, who would look after me.

Late that evening I took my anti-depressant, which I had dubbed my happy pills, and promptly stayed awake most of the night. I assumed that it was simply a case of feeling more positive as a result of having done something about the depression. The next night I took the tablet at the same time and again stayed awake all night. As Ray was on holiday I couldn't ring him up to ask him what he thought might be going on so I decided to follow my hunch and took the anti-depressant the next morning. I didn't feel tired all day and slept like a log that night. I continued to take my tablet every morning and everything seemed to be fine. A few days later I was lying in bed one night with my head on one side on the pillow when I realised I could hear my heart beating extremely fast. I thought nothing of it and promptly fell asleep. It was a week later that I had an appointment with Dr O'Connor at the hospital. We were talking about how the MS symptoms were and I told him that Ray had put me on anti-depressants at my request. "Good idea," said Dr O'Connor with his famous grin. I then told him that I thought my pulse was a bit fast. He came round to where I was sitting at the other side of his desk and took my wrist in order to check my pulse. He didn't even bother to time it but looked up at me with raised eyebrows and said, "You're right. That is fast!" He sat down again and scribbled a note in my file and said, "I think we'll put you on a tranquilliser to slow that down." "On your bike!" I responded with a chuckle. "I'm not taking an anti-depressant to boost me up only for you to slam me on tranquillisers to knock me down again." He grinned and said to a registrar who was there, "See what I'm up against? She bullies me." Dr O'Connor then told me that he was going to be away for the next three weeks and introduced me to his registrar who would be there if I needed steroids or anything else.

I went home on wobbly legs feeling as if it was "abandon Cari time" with both Ray and Dr O'Connor being away. Later that evening I sat down on the floor and rang my Mum to give her an update on my progress and to tell her how things had gone with Dr O'Connor. An hour later I hung up and struggled to my feet to go and put the phone away. As I stood up something felt strange. "Shit. What's gone wrong now?" I thought. I systematically checked out my knees, back and balance. No, that was all the same as usual. Over the next ten minutes the truth began to dawn on me. What felt strange was that I was back to normal! I couldn't believe what was happening. I tried running on the spot and found that I could do it. I could actually make my legs move as fast as I wanted. I then tried to do something that slow responses, weakness in my legs and loss of balance had made impossible for twenty-two months. I danced. "My god," I thought, "I can damn well do it!" At that moment *Top of the Pops* began on the television and for fifteen minutes I danced in front of the mirror in my flat for the sheer joy of it. I laughed out loud as I watched myself dancing dressed only in T-shirt and knickers. I am not sure that I had ever previously felt as happy as I did then. It was a miracle. It was all I had never dared to hope for. I was back to normal.

I finally collapsed on the floor, out of breath, but deliriously happy. I started to think about what was happening to me. My first thought was, "This won't last of course", but I reckoned that if I could repeat the experience for just one hour a week then I could handle having MS. At least I would know from time to time that the real Cari was still there. I was sure that within an hour I would be back to square one again or, at the very best, it would last until I went to bed but I would wake up in the morning with the physical problems again. I knew that my return to full ability was simply not possible, there was too much nerve damage for even a spontaneous remission to allow full recovery. My researcher's mind clicked in at the point. "If I have done anything to make this happen" I thought "Then I *have* to work out what it is so I can do it again." I began to work things through. "What's the new variable in the situation?" I wondered. "What have I done that I had never done before?" That was easy, I had started taking an anti-depressant ten days ago. That was my first starting point. I got out a book, the *Mimms* drugs directory, that my best friend Colm had lent me when he knew I was gong on to anti-depressant so I could read up about them. I turned to the page on my anti-depressant. Hmmm . . . nothing much there. Then I turned to the page describing the mechanism of the particular type of drug I was on. "These drugs work by inhibiting the reabsorption of noradrenaline into the pre-synaptic cleft," I read. Feeling speedy? Moving faster? Noradrenaline . . . sounds like adrenalin, I thought. Surely it couldn't be *that* easy. I went to bed and lay there hugging myself and grinning like an idiot. I loved my body for the first time in twenty-two months. It had come back to me, it was on my side again. I marvelled at how amazing the human body is when it works properly. It had never occurred to me prior to developing MS that having a fully functional body is the most amazing thing in the world. We all take it for granted, until it fails that is. That was a realisation that I knew I would never forget. *Nothing* else in life truly matters as long as your body works. It doesn't matter if you are less than beautiful, or overweight, just so long as your body works. I knew at that moment that I would never feel bad about my body again. 19 August 1994 was a day I knew I would never forget for as long as I lived.

The next day I woke up and was thrilled to discover that the improvement had sustained. I jumped out of bed and jogged through the flat to the bathroom. I still couldn't stop grinning. I began to think I would never be able to wipe that smile off my face. I went to work and spent the morning bouncing around showing people what had happened overnight. My colleagues couldn't believe what they were seeing. I jumped up and down in front of them and hopped and ran and generally showed off. I was incapable of walking down a corridor. I ran everywhere. I was still convinced that the improvement wouldn't last and so was determined to make the most of it. I discovered that I could run upstairs but, when I tried to run back down again, I found that my leg muscles were still too weak to make that possible. It was another eight months before I was able to safely run downstairs. Later that morning I rang Hilary to tell her about my miraculous recovery. She was obviously thrilled but then said, "Do you remember what you told me you were doing a few weeks ago just before your flood?" I had been plea bargaining with God. "Good grief," I said "I was asking for a positive sign." "Heh. That's spooky," I shrieked. Hilary laughed and said, "Well. God *does* act in strange ways sometimes." I brushed that off and told her that I thought it was something to do with the action of the anti-depressants. This was no miracle. I was determined to prove that it was something *I* had done.

I then rang the registrar at the hospital who was looking after me in Dr O'Connor's absence. I told him what had happened and that I was now able to run. "Are you sure, Cari?" he asked. "Sure." I replied. "Would I joke about something like this?" I then asked him about the anti-depressant I was on and asked him if he thought it could be responsible for my improvement. "No way," he said "Hundreds of people with MS take that drug and if it did anything for symptoms we would have seen it by now." Oh well, there went that bright idea.

That afternoon I connected to Lambda MOO, a virtual reality network on the computer Internet that is run by the Xerox Corporation in America. I had been connecting to Lambda from time to time over the previous six months since I discovered it. Lambda allows people from all over the world to communicate to each other in real time by typing and reading each others words on the screen. I had made many friends on Lambda and they all knew about the fact that I had MS. No one on Lambda knows who anyone else is in real life as we all have names that we made up. At that time my character was Britgirl although I later changed it to Lecturer. These complete strangers had been amazingly supportive to me when I was feeling low and needed someone to "talk" to. I even had a friend, whose character was a horse, who would give me virtual reality rides when I was having trouble walking! This friend, Nearco, who is in California, described his character as "A large brown horse, standing nearly seventeen hands high. His large brown eyes gaze at you with a look of sly intelligence. He is a deep mahogany bay with a long black mane and tail and black points. Powerful muscles ripple beneath his skin." It was funny, if a little weird, to be pretending to ride when I could barely walk. Lambda had become my alternative social life when I wasn't physically able to get out and meet people and, in virtual reality, disabilities didn't matter.

I had also met a guy from America, called Malibu, who had Cystic Fibrosis and was bed-bound and on oxygen twenty-four hours a day but who still managed to use Lambda as a way of communicating with people. He and I talked a lot about how useful Lambda was for people with disabilities who often end up isolated. I also met up with a lady who was blind but had an adaptation to her computer that allowed her to speak and translated that into typed words for others to read and which "spoke" the words when someone else typed them on the screen. There were an amazing number of people on Lambda with disabilities. We decided that all hospital wards ought to have computer links to Lambda for people to use while they were hospitalised.

I decided that I had to share my joy with my virtual reality friends. I was "talking" to several of my friends who happened to be connected at the same time. One of my best friends, BenD, who I think was in Australia, was there. He asked me how I was feeling generally and I told him that I felt great but that I had noticed that my pulse was unusually fast. "How fast is it?" he typed. "I don't know," I responded "I haven't taken my pulse :)." In computer talk :) is a smiley. Tip your head to the left to look at it and you will see what it means. "Take it now," appeared on my screen. Using the digital clock on my computer screen I counted my pulse for a minute and typed "It's 120". "WHAT?!" BenD flashed on to my screen. "Is that fast then?" I typed. I laughed out loud when I saw what BenD had typed next, "!! GET TO A DOCTOR NOW !!". "OK OK," I responded "Sheesh. There's no need to shout! :)". "I'm serious," typed BenD "That is nearly double what it should be." That took me by surprise so I decided to follow his advice.

The next morning I was due to go to the doctor's surgery to get my B12 injection which I was having a ten week course of. B12 doesn't actually do anything beneficial for MS but neurologists tend to give it to people anyway. It is sometimes used to treat sub-acute spinal degeneration and was once thought to help the nerves damaged by MS to repair themselves. It is known by those of us with MS as the consultant's consolation prize. It won't do any good but neither will it do any harm, and at least we get some attention once a week for ten weeks. When I was called in by Sally, the nursing sister, I told her that I had noticed that my pulse was rather fast. She took it and looked worried. Then she took my blood pressure and looked even more concerned. "I'm not going to give you your B12 until a doctor has seen you," she said. I shrugged, not in the least concerned. After a few minutes Michael came down and took my pulse and blood pressure. "I'm not happy with this," he said. "Look," I replied. "Sinus Tachycardia (benign fast heart beat) is a known side effect of these anti-depressants." He got out his drug book and looked up the anti-depressant I was on. "How did you know that?" he asked, so I told him that I had looked it up the night before. Michael was not at all happy about my pulse rate and told me that I must stop taking the anti-depressants and that I must have an ECG that afternoon. I smiled, having no intention of stopping taking my pills, as I was sure they had something to do with my miraculous recovery. Michael gave me a form to take to a local hospital for an ECG that afternoon and told me to come back and see him the next morning. "If they find something wrong with your heart they will admit you and control it with drugs," he said. I replied, "No one puts me on any drug without Dr O'Connor agreeing to it first. And he is on holiday." Michael repeated that if there was a problem I would have no say in the matter. As he had never dealt with me before he couldn't possibly know how silly that statement was. I grinned evilly at him and said, "Don't you believe it my friend," turned on my heel and walked out.

I duly turned up at the hospital at one o'clock and, after a short wait I was wired up to an ECG machine and the test was run. It only took a few minutes and they asked me to go back to the waiting room where I would be given my results. I waited for about quarter of an hour and finally a nurse came out with the printout of the ECG and told me that I should give it to my GP but that I could go. Written on the top of the trace were the words "Sinus Tachycardia" which made me chuckle. The next morning I went back to see Michael as arranged and handed over the ECG result saying airily, "See. I told you so." He took my pulse again, which was still 120, and said, "I think you ought to come back tomorrow morning and see if it has dropped now you are off the anti-depressants" but I hadn't got the heart to tell him that I hadn't stopped taking them. So I went back the following morning and he once again took my pulse. The poor boy was getting quite upset that my pulse wasn't returning to normal and decided to take a blood test to see if I had a thyroid problem. I was beginning to feel guilty about not telling him the truth because he was being so kind and concerned about me. The next morning when I had to go back again to see him I finally owned up. "I'm sorry Michael," I said "I haven't been exactly honest with you. I never stopped taking my anti-depressants." He was very good and didn't even tell me off. He suggested I waited until Ray came back from holiday and spoke to him about it. This was the point at which my life began to get, as I would refer to it down the line, "seriously spooky".

✦

CHAPTER FIVE

FROM BREAKDOWN TO
BREAKTHROUGH

✦

I HAD already looked up my anti-depressant in the drug book that Colm had lent me but had not, as yet, looked at another one on amino acids which he had given me to see if I would be interested in using amino acids to come off the anti-depressants in due course. He had helped cut down the dose of his mother's anti-depressants by using an amino acid. I had just arrived at work one day and saw the book lying on my desk. I picked it up and began idly to leaf through it. Suddenly I came across a page labelled with one of the contents of cola. "What the hell is an amino acid doing in cola?" I thought. I read that page and then looked up the amino acid in the index. There was one more reference to it so I turned to that page. I read the brief statement which said something along the lines of "If you are taking (a different type of anti-depressant) you should not supplement with this amino acid as it boosts the levels of circulating adrenalin." I sat there thinking "Bingo. That's it!. My anti-depressant and cola cures MS!" I sat there giggling at how stupid that was for a moment and then got serious and turned my mind to trying to work out what it might be doing to bypass the nerve damage caused by MS. All I could imagine was that the adrenalin was making the nerves fire faster.

Ray had just come back from holiday and I had arranged to see him the next day. I assumed that he knew nothing about what had happened while he had been on holiday and, as it happens, I was correct. He came down to the waiting room to collect me and, as he always did, ran up the stairs to his office in front of me. That had always annoyed me as I struggled up the stairs after him, so this time I decided to play him at his own game. He had gone up about four steps when I started to run up after him. He got to the top of the flight of stairs and turned round looking at me in amazement. "What *have* you done?" he asked. I grinned at him and said "Ahh . . . now that's quite a story."

We went and sat down in his office and I told him the story of my symptoms going away in the blink of an eye, my pulse being fast, having an ECG and the fact that it showed Sinus Tachycardia. I then explained to him what I thought was going on in terms of the higher adrenalin levels making the nerves fire faster. "Nerves don't work like that," said Ray. "They are like switches, either on or off. You can't make them switch faster." "Damn," I thought. "Yet another bright idea thrown out of the window." "But," said Ray "you could be making the fight or flight response nerve fibres fire." He got out his prescription pad and started to draw a diagram on the back of it. He talked me through the fact that the fight or flight response nerve fibres are in the centre of the nerve axon and, therefore, are away from the part of the nerve that MS attacks (the myelin sheath). These fibres have a higher firing potentiality (they are fired by higher levels of adrenalin) and, as my treatment was boosting the levels of adrenalin, this was likely to be what was going on. He offered to lend me his physiology textbooks from his medical student days so I could read up on the structure and function of nerves. He explained to me that there was a possibility that the nerve fibres could get used to the higher levels of adrenalin and would consequently "up the anti" and the effect I was seeing would wear off. He reminded me of an example of this. If you go into a room where there is a bad smell, after a while you cease to smell it. We both agreed that only time would tell. I then said, "Look, I don't care what you say, I am not going to stop taking these drugs, but what risks am I running in making my heart beat faster?" "None really," he replied "You are just exercising the heart muscles." He said it would be a good idea if I had my pulse and blood pressure checked each time that I had my B12 injection so he could monitor what was going on. I nodded and then grinned at him and said "Do you remember when I asked for anti-depressants I said that I wanted a holiday from MS?" "Yes," he said "And I said that I couldn't do that." We grinned at each other, both thinking the same thing. Against the odds that is exactly what I had got.

Next I decided that I needed to know exactly how much of the amino acid I was getting from drinking a litre and a half of cola a day because, as it stood, I had absolutely no idea. I rang up a freephone consumer number and asked them if they could tell me. "Why do you need to know?" the lady asked me "Is it because of a medical condition?" "Yes" I replied. She then said that she could not tell me but that she would let the head office know and they would get in touch with me. A week later I received a letter from them telling me that they were not at liberty to disclose the information I had requested but that, if I wanted to take the matter further, they would pass the request on to another person there. I felt frustrated at not being able to find out the information I so desperately needed and, consequently, logged on to Lambda to moan about the way I was being thwarted. I was "talking" to a few friends when a character, Mollusc, whom I had never communicated with before, joined in the conversation. "What's all this about?" he typed. I explained briefly and ended up by saying, "And no one will tell me." "I can do that for you," he typed. "WHAT? You mean you can analyse it for me?" I flashed up on the screen. "Hang on," he said, "I can calculate it." I waited for a few minutes, watching the screen with baited breath. Suddenly the words I had been waiting for appeared. "You are taking in about a gram a day of the amino acid," wrote Mollusc. "Hell. That's not much," I typed, feeling let down. "WHAT?" wrote Mollusc. "That is a hell of a lot of an amino acid!" It transpired that Mollusc was a twenty-one-year-old food technologist working in New Zealand.

As a result of Mollusc telling me how much of the amino acid I was getting from the cola I was able to go to my chemist and ask him if it was possible to get the amino acid in tablets. He looked it up in his drug book and confirmed that it was available in capsules at the right dose so I could take it twice a day. He told me that he would fax an order in for me and it should arrive the next morning, which it did. I had decided that it was essential to isolate the amino acid from the cola to make sure that it really was the active ingredient in my treatment. From the next day when I picked up my capsules I came off all soft drinks and drank only water. The treatment seemed to work even better when using the capsules, so I was certain that I had the theory right.

The next thing I did was to try to make sure that my improvement was due to the treatment and not simply an amazing remission. I was more inclined to accept that I had been misdiagnosed with MS than I was to seriously believe that I had found a solution to it. As I was an empirical researcher I decided to go without one or the other or both drugs on four separate occasions to see if it made any difference to my physical condition. Two days after getting my capsules I took one in the morning but left out the anti-depressant. Much to my amazement I was having trouble walking again by lunchtime. "Maybe it's psychosomatic," I pondered. The next morning I took both drugs and within two hours I could run upstairs again. A week or so later I took the anti-depressant but left out the amino acid. Again by lunchtime my symptoms were returning. I repeated the experiment on two further occasions with the same outcome each time. I was finally convinced that my treatment was indeed responsible for my miraculous improvement.

To this day I can't get over the coincidence of Mollusc and I being connected to Lambda at the same time. The time difference between New Zealand and the UK made the chance of us both being connected simultaneously quite slim. When I looked at Mollusc's description I should not have been surprised that he had been so willing to help me. It read, "A tall slim man, with a quiet and hesitant manner at first. He is intensely shy, probably because he is so unsure of himself. He proudly displays Mollusc's Official Helpful Person Badge." From that day Mollusc and I tried to make sure that we met up regularly. That meant me going to work at seven o'clock in the morning and him staying late at work, as Auckland is eleven hours ahead of the UK. We began to discuss how the drug mechanism could be working and how I could develop my theory further. Mollusc had access to the *Merck Index* and he looked up all the drugs in my cocktail for me. Gradually the biochemical explanation started to emerge. My research began to confirm what Ray and I had worked out. It was an exciting and fascinating process of mutual discovery. My mind was going into overdrive as I made more and more connections through understanding the bio-chemistry. I began to think further and ask myself more questions about the possible action of the treatment. Nearly every morning I would race to the office and connect to Lambda in the hope of meeting up with Mollusc. I always had another idea to put to him or another question to ask. We were a damned good research team although we had never met in real life or even spoken on the phone.

One day Mollusc and I were typing away to each other when I happened to mention that a contact of mine in a national newspaper had said that he would like to run the story of my discovery. "Guess what," I typed "The press want to take my story!" One of my Lambda pals in the UK, Hookleg, was listening in as Mollusc and I communicated. He suddenly typed, "Keep you mouth shut girl. PATENT IT." "What?" I responded. "I can't patent this, I haven't created anything." "Oh yes you can," responded Hookleg, "You must file the Intellectual Property Rights before you allow anything to be published." "He's right," added Mollusc "If this is for real it could be huge." I didn't quite know what to make of that. I hadn't done anything, it was all pure chance. It transpired that Hookleg was a PhD student in genetics at Leicester University but, before he became a research student, he had been a trainee patent lawyer so he knew what he was talking about. I pondered the idea for a while and then decided to try and do something about it.

During the course of my career at the Institute of Education I had worked on a piece of research looking at business funding of higher education and, consequently, knew a few contacts in the university world who had dealings with Intellectual Property Rights. I rang one of them, Allen, and briefly explained to him the situation and said, "I can't file a patent on that can I?" "You certainly can," replied Allen "And what is more you must!" He put me in touch with the patent lawyer that his university used and told me that the lawyer would probably do me the same cut-price financial deal if I mentioned where the contact had come from. I was very unsure about launching into the world of filing a biochemical patent. I felt completely out of my depth and was sure that I would achieve nothing more than making a fool of myself. I rang Peter, the Director of the Institute of Education, to tell him what I was doing with the patenting as I thought he might be interested. He was delighted and asked me how much it was going to cost to do the filing. I told him that it should be in the region of 300 pounds at which point he said "We will pay for that just to show our support for you. I'll arrange for a cheque to be made out for you." I was stunned. It hadn't occurred to me to ask the Institute to provide any money. I thanked him profusely not knowing quite what to say.

Later that same day I summoned up the courage to ring John, the patent lawyer. I got straight through to him and hesitantly explained my situation. "What do you think?" I asked. "Is it possible to patent something like this?" "Certainly," replied John. "Although I have to tell you that you have picked one of the most difficult domains to cut your teeth on!" Apparently filing medical drugs patents is one of the most notoriously difficult areas there is. John said he would do me the same cut-price deal as the university but that I would have to write the patent statement myself. "Oh sure," I thought. "Dream on." I really didn't believe that my A level biology and chemistry would stand me in a particularly good position to be able to pull that off. John told me that he would send me some literature about patenting to get me started. I found a copy of a patent statement in the package that John sent me and simply copied the format for my own one. I started off with the title "A New Therapeutic Treatment for Multiple Sclerosis and other Demyelinating Diseases". There, that looked official enough. It was nowhere near as difficult as I had imagined it would be and I completed writing it in about half an hour.

On 30 September I had an appointment to see Dr O'Connor for the first time since he came back from holiday. It was another teaching session so I decided in advance that I would put on a real show for them. After a longish wait I was called into the lecture theatre. I bounced through the doorway and up to Dr O'Connor's desk smiling like an idiot. Dr O'Connor looked rather surprised at my agility and grinning said "And how are you then? Had more steroids while I was away I assume?" "Nope," I replied. "I haven't had any since I saw you in July." "Really?" he said. "Well you are looking well." "Ahh," I said grinning at him. "I'll tell you about that in a minute." He put me through the regular tests for balance, limb strength and coordination, checked my eyes and reflexes and commented that I was doing very well indeed. We sat down again at his desk and he said, "Come on then. What have you done." I handed over a copy of my newly drafted patent statement and ran through the explanation of my magic treatment at breakneck pace. Dr O'Connor picked up the paper and waved it in the air to the SHOs, saying "This is her thesis you know." "Don't be silly," I retorted. "It's my patent statement." Dr O'Connor grinned broadly and turned to the SHOs again and said "OK but it's still her thesis." He then said to me "Now. Tell me again. It is the noradrenaline that is making the nerves work?" "ADrenalin," I said "And its firing the fight or flight response nerve fibres." We talked it through a bit longer while he struggled with the theory. "What do you think then?" I asked finally. "I don't know," he said. "I'll have to read it through properly." "OK," I replied. "But I know that it is working." Dr O'Connor then addressed the SHOs again and said, "I shouldn't be surprised. She's already worked out how to use the steroids differently and it worked for her." We agreed to meet again in two months' time and I left the hospital feeling pretty chuffed.

Dr O'Connor wrote to Ray after that meeting saying:

I was delighted to see that Miss Loder is in remission and has not required any intravenous Prednisolone for nine weeks. She has evolved a rather complex theory that it was the amino acid in her cola that has helped make her better by causing the blood flow in her brain to bypass the plaques of demyelination. I will have to study her theory in detail to comment upon it.

He had completely misunderstood my theory!

I continued to stay well with no physical deterioration or recurrence of the MS when, out of the blue, I was taken ill in the early hours of the morning on Sunday 2 October. I had been having stomach pains and discomfort since ten o'clock that night and by two o'clock in the morning I was fed up with not being able to get comfortable enough to sleep so I called out a

GP. She arrived and asked me what the problem was. Before she arrived I had looked up my symptoms in the *Oxford Handbook of Clinical Medicine* and was pretty sure that I had cholecystitis or, in other words, gallstones. I explained what had been happening since ten o'clock that night and the doctor prodded my stomach. "You've got gallstones" she said gravely. I grinned and said, "I thought as much." She opened her case and said, "I'll give you Pethidine for the pain". "Don't be daft," I retorted. "It's not bad enough to warrant that and I haven't even taken Paracetamol for it yet." She looked confused and said "But gallstones cause the worst pain known to mankind!" "Maybe," I replied. "But it is not bothering me unduly." She seemed upset and asked me if I would at least allow her to give me an injection of an anti-spasmodic. I agreed just to keep her happy. She left after instructing me to deliver myself to the surgery first thing in the morning to see Ray.

At nine o'clock on Monday morning, after a night with no sleep, I went to see Ray and arrived at the surgery before he did. He turned up a few minutes later to find me sitting on the bottom step of the stairs leading up to his office. He did a double take and said, "Hello. What are you doing here?" "I've got gallstones," I said. "I saw a GP last night and she told me to come and see you this morning." "Come on up to my office," Ray said. "I can't climb the stairs," I replied. "I'm knackered." Ray took me into an examination room on the ground floor and poked my stomach. "OK," he said, "I'll give you a shot of Pethidine." I told him that I had refused it from the GP the night before but he looked at me and said "You are getting Pethidine *now*." I grinned, knowing I had no choice. What Ray says goes and I knew better than to argue. He disappeared for a moment and then came back to give me my injection. "Stay here," said Ray after he had injected me, "and I'll come back and see you in a while." I had no intention of hanging around as I was starting to teach a new course on the Wednesday and I had to get back to work to deliver the course handbook to the printers. I explained that to Ray and he said, "You are not going anywhere for at least an hour." I grumbled a bit and told him that I would wait for half an hour anyway. Ten minutes later he returned and told me that he had rung the hospital and that I had to deliver myself to Accident and Emergency by eleven o'clock that morning and that I would be admitted. "They aren't going to operate are they?" I asked. "Maybe," said Ray. "But you will need twenty-four hour a day analgesia anyway."

Ray realised that I was still fretting about getting back to work and that he was unlikely to be able to make me stay in the surgery much longer, so he took me by the arm and led me out of the examination room. "That," he said, pointing, "is a phone. You can call whoever you want to let people know what's going on. But *please* sit down when you are making your calls." "OK," I replied and promptly stood there phoning people for the next twenty minutes organising people to take over my work at the office and letting Hilary know that I was about to be admitted to hospital. An hour after having given me the Pethidine, Ray came back down and handed me a letter to take to A and E. He told me that I had to get a taxi there and that on no account was I to walk down the road. I told him that I had to drop in at the office first and then I had to go home to pack a bag if I was going to be admitted to the hospital. He said that was fine but reiterated that I *must* not walk anywhere as Pethidine makes people go a bit strange and I wouldn't be safe walking around on the street. I then realised that I had left my bag at the office and didn't have any money which I told Ray. He promptly pulled out a twenty-pound note and handed it to me saying, "You can give that back when all this is over." He also asked me to ring him from the hospital the next day to tell him how things were going.

I left the surgery and promptly walked back to the office as I felt fine and didn't see any point in hanging around for a taxi. I sorted things out at work and went home to pack a bag and finally presented myself at the hospital just before eleven o'clock. I was dealt with immediately and had to get undressed, put on a hospital gown and wait on a trolley in a cubicle. From time to time a registrar, SHO, houseman or nurse would come in and take my blood pressure, or set up a drip or take my temperature. At one point a newly qualified houseman came in to set up a drip as the rule, until they had sorted me out, would be nil by mouth. We chatted as he sorted out the equipment and I told him which were the best veins in the back of my hand to try for. I was something of an expert on Venflons by then due to the number of steroid drips I had been given. He seemed to appreciate my help and tried to put the Venflon in, but failed. We talked it through and had a few abortive attempts before he decided to call the registrar to do it. Finally the drip was put in successfully and I was once again left alone.

In due course an SHO, Neil, came in and said, "I'm sorry we have kept you waiting so long but we have found a bed for you now". "That's OK," I replied. "It hasn't been that long." Neil looked at me quizzically and asked, "Have you had Pethidine this morning by any chance?" "Sure," I said. "I had a shot at nine o'clock before I came here." He chuckled and said, "What time do you think it is, Cari?" "Well," I said, "I was admitted at eleven o'clock so it must be getting on for twelve now." Neil laughed and said, "I see. You're going to be someone who likes Pethidine." I asked him what on earth he meant. He finally told me that it was a quarter to four in the afternoon! I had no idea that so much time had passed as the Pethidine had completely destroyed my sense of time. Quite a bonus seeing as I had been lying on a trolley for four and three quarter hours without being bored for a second.

I was taken up to the ward and Neil came to my bedside to have a chat about what was likely to happen. "The first thing," he said, "is that you can have nothing to eat or drink until we have got you sorted out." I told him that I had to continue taking my tablets twice a day. He asked me what I was taking and when I explained he asked me why on earth I was taking that combination. I explained about the MS and what my treatment did for me. "You aren't going to stop taking those," he said. I very patronisingly put my hand on his arm and said, "How right you are. I'm glad we aren't going to have a fight about this." "No," he said, "I'm *telling* you. You aren't going to stop taking them." I was somewhat bemused and asked him why he felt that way. He looked at me and said, "You are not going to muck around with the MS while you are in here." He asked me to explain how I thought the treatment was working, so I ran through the mechanism as far as I had worked it out. His jaw dropped and he said, "Oh shit. Well it *would*. Why didn't *we* think of that!"

The next day I was transferred to a nearby hospital and I spent the next three days causing quite a stir with the medics. The story of me and my MS treatment had spread around the hospital and, from time to time, an SHO, houseman or registrar would come and find me to hear the story first-hand. I was having great fun trying out my theory on them and hearing their responses. They all responded the same, wondering why someone hadn't thought of it before. I had keyhole surgery late on Thursday afternoon to remove my gall bladder which by then we knew had a stone the size of a golfball in it, very inflamed and infected. The surgery was uneventful as far as I was concerned and I finally came to properly at about midnight. The first thing I wanted was a drink as I had not been able to eat or drink anything since the previous Sunday night. The nurse brought me a glass of fresh orange juice which tasted like nectar to me. I had no post-operative pain and slept soundly through the night despite being roused every hour by the nurses who had to take my pulse, blood pressure and temperature.

The next day Neil came to see me to report on the operation and to see how I was feeling. "Well," he said. "You won't have any more problems from your gall bladder. It was the most revoltingly disgusting thing I have ever seen. It had no business being inside a living person!" I chuckled and told him not to be rude. He then said "Now . . . how's the MS holding up?" I told him that it was fine and hadn't flickered once through the entire episode. He nodded as if that was what he had been expecting to hear and said, "You do realise that your treatment must not only be bypassing the nerve damage but protecting you from further attack as well, don't you?" I giggled helplessly at him and said, "Oh sure. Pull the other one!" He smiled and said, "You have faced five of the known major triggers for MS attack this week. No food or drink, systemic infection, intravenous antibiotics, major surgery and deep anaesthesia. Do you have a better explanation as to why you haven't had an attack?" That pulled me up short so I shrugged and told him I guessed he must be right. I still thought it was hysterically funny though. There's no way the solution to such a complex incurable disease could be so simple.

I was discharged from the hospital on Saturday evening and as soon as I got home I ordered a Chinese takeaway which I had been dreaming about for days. The next morning I went in to work to see what I had been missing while I was in hospital and discovered, much to my surprise, that no problems awaited me. On Monday morning, exactly a week after I had been admitted to hospital, I went in to see Ray to tell him that I was out of hospital. He was stunned to see me as he didn't know I was going to have keyhole surgery and, therefore, expected me to be in hospital for a couple of weeks. He was delighted that the MS had held steady all the way through the ordeal. I told him what Neil had said about my treatment protecting me from attacks and Ray agreed that he might be correct. I had missed the last injection of B12 while I was in hospital but I thought it was worth finishing the course so I got Sally, the nursing sister, to give me the injection after I saw Ray.

Two weeks later I was sitting at my desk at work one afternoon when I realised that my right arm was tingling and that the left side of my face had gone numb. I began to get upset as I realised the MS was back for the first time in two months. "Oh shit," I thought. "I've made a fool of myself. It was only ever a remission. So much for my happy pills and cola." Then I remembered my trial with stopping and starting the drugs and realised that it could not have been simply a remission. Twenty minutes later I was fine again and so dismissed the episode as a minor glitch. Over the next three or four days the tingling and numbness happened again and my left knee started to give way when I was walking. I switched into researcher mode and went back to my original starting point in August, "What had I done that I had never done before?" As soon as I thought that I knew the answer. It wasn't a case of what had I done, it was what had I *stopped* doing. I had not had the B12 for two weeks. I went back to see Sally the next morning with the intention of asking her if I could have another shot of B12 to see what happened. Sally wasn't sure but said she would ask Ray for me. She came back a minute later, having spoken to Ray, and told me that he had said that he had no idea whether it would do anything for me but that it was certainly worth a try and I seemed to have a pretty good idea about what I was doing. I had my B12 shot and an hour later all my symptoms had gone again!

And so started the next leg on my journey of discovery. Researching B12, I could not find anything that made much sense except that it might be making the amino acid work better. I kept mulling it over but was getting nowhere. A few days later I was sitting at home watching television when I felt an itch on my right forearm and went to scratch it. This in itself was not significant except for the fact that I realised for the first time since starting on my treatment that a skin condition I had developed on both forearms in the summer of 1984 was clear. It had only ever got better when I was having the two weekly intravenous steroids for the MS and had returned when I stopped having steroids. Now it was clear again. "Don't tell me my treatment is having a steroidal effect!" I thought. It certainly seemed as if something was acting like steroids do in terms of being powerful anti-inflammatory drugs. That would certainly account for why I was being protected from further attacks. I began reading up about the three drugs again and discovered that all three of them had one thing in common. All the molecules contained benzene rings in their structure. From my A level chemistry I knew that benzene rings were highly volatile and so began to wonder if the molecules were linking and, perhaps, creating a steroidal molecule.

The next morning I raced to the office and hit Lambda in the hope that Mollusc would be connected. I was desperate to ask him what he thought of my theory. Thankfully he connected to Lambda a few minutes after I did. The second he connected I slammed him with my theory and asked him what he thought. There was much mutual hmmming and ahhhing and we spent several minutes typing "Gosh, I don't know" and "Something is happening" to each other. Mollusc was quiet for a while and then suddenly typed "BLOODY HELL!" "What what what??" I responded, almost bouncing up and down in my chair in excitement. "The benzene rings are blasting the molecules apart and the parts are relinking and are making a lipophobic macro steroidal molecule!!" Mollusc wrote. I asked him to translate that as I was unsure what the words meant. He explained that a very large molecule that looked just like a steroid was being made but that it was water-soluble and, therefore, was almost certainly non-toxic. Steroids are highly toxic as they are stored in the body fat and accumulate over time. If a steroid were water soluble it would not build up in the body and would simply be flushed out. We both sat there at opposite sides of the world staring at the words on our screens and not believing what we might have discovered. We were so excited that we could barely type coherently. "I might be wrong of course," typed Mollusc. "But it is certainly making something pretty close to that." I could have hugged him and I felt that I simply *had* to talk to him on the phone. I got him to give me the phone number where he was at that moment and I rang up Auckland. He answered the phone instantly and I said, "Mollusc? It's Britgirl." We spent a couple of minutes being able to say little more than "This is weird. You are actually real!" to each other. We briefly discussed what we might have discovered and how amazing it was that we had done the whole thing through Lambda. As it was quite an expensive call we only talked for a few minutes and I hung up. I sat at my desk grinning at having finally got to talk to my mate Mollusc in real life.

Two weeks after having been discharged from the hospital I went back to the outpatients' clinic for a follow-up. Neil saw me and asked me how I had been, checked how the cuts were healing and said that I had made a very good recovery and promptly discharged me from the hospital. He also wrote to Ray:

As you know Cari has recently been an in-patient here after an acute episode of cholecystitis. Since then she has made an extremely good rapid recovery. Her multiple sclerosis seems to be completely stable at present. On examination today the wound has healed extremely well. She is back to full activity. The histology revealed this to be an acute chronic cholecystitis with ulceration of the gall bladder.

When I next saw Ray he commented on the letter and the fact that I had healed so quickly. I then told him all about the theory of the steroidal molecule and he said, "That could explain why you healed so fast." "Good grief," I thought "Maybe this is for real." I began to think about all the illnesses that could be treated if we really had discovered a non-toxic steroid. Asthma could be treated prophylactically, psoriasis should respond to it, in fact anything for which steroids can only be used sparingly due to the toxic side effects, could benefit. The fact that my happy pills and cola interacted to bypass the MS nerve damage was a mind blowing enough coincidence but the fact that the B12 was part of the treatment as well freaked me out.

That was the point at which I started to think that too many coincidences were happening to be believed. It felt as if everything that was happening was meant to be, that someone had put down a paper trail and I was simply following it. That was the moment that I began to believe that a guiding force was using me. I didn't feel comfortable relating to the power as "God". I decided, out of the blue, that I would think of the power as the northern lights. The northern lights are beautiful, immensely powerful and mysterious. That appealed to me. That night I saw on television, for the first time, an advertisement for shares in an electricity company. The image that was used was that of the northern lights. I sat there watching it thinking "Now *that's* spooky." It almost felt as if the power was telling me that it was alright to relate to it in that way. I saw the advert every day until, one evening, I was talking to Hilary and told her about naming the power the northern lights and seeing the advert for the first time. Hilary reckoned that it didn't matter what you called the power so long as you were in touch with it. That night the advert came on but they had changed the image. I felt as if I was being told that I had got the message and so it was not necessary to repeat it. I believed without a shadow of a doubt, from that moment on, that I was indeed being used.

As the patent had been filed for me by John, my patent agent, while I was in hospital having my gall bladder removed I was safe to release the information to drug companies to see if I could persuade one of them to take the patent and conduct clinical trials. I contacted all the major drug companies, Glaxo, Wellcome, SmithKline Beecham, Merck, Novo Nordisk and several others; they all asked me to send them my patent statement. After a couple of weeks I began to receive letters telling me that they did not feel able to take the patent for various reasons, the most common being that it fell outside of their brief. Only one gave a different reason which they refused to put in writing for me but which they read out to me over the phone. They said that their biochemists had confirmed that the drugs would indeed have the effect that I claimed and that they could easily blister pack the drugs and sell them as a treatment for MS. The problem was that they knew that as soon as their product fell into the GPs' hands they would see the contents and promptly prescribe the generic versions. Consequently the drug company felt that there was not a sufficiently high profit in it for them to warrant taking the patent. I should have been incensed that a drug company could see that there was a potentially effective treatment for MS but that they would not touch it due to purely financial reasons. As it was, I was thrilled that I had received confirmation from the biochemists that my theory about the interaction was correct. I battled on with the other companies until one day I received a letter from one of them saying they were very interested. I rang them up and had a long talk about the theory and my observations. Over the next two weeks I had almost daily phone calls with my contact, Steve, as the patent progressed through their research, development and financial boards. I was getting increasingly excited about the prospect of getting them to take the patent on. One morning I spoke to Steve and he told me that their Director of Neurochemistry had reservations about my patent and felt that he needed evidence that it would work for other people. I rang him up and he suggested that I get five or six other people on my treatment and give him the results when I had them. I was overwhelmed at the prospect of running my own clinical trial but I knew that I had no choice if I wanted to get the treatment taken seriously and also if I wanted to prove to myself that my treatment was the true cause of my recovery. And so began the most chaotic and astonishing period of my life that I had ever had to deal with.

◆

CHAPTER SIX

HOPE IS HELL

◆

BY NOW it was March 1995 and, as a result of the drug company involvement, I had started to wonder how I was going to get people on to my treatment. The first person, Gill, found her way to me through a very tenuous thread. I had been acting as a rapporteur (the person who summarises the debate) for Patrick, the director of an important national think-tank, the previous December where he had told people about my miraculous recovery. Patrick had known me before and during the MS and was a very good friend of mine so he was thrilled to death when I recovered and was excited, to say the least, about the fact that I had apparently developed an effective treatment. In January I had received a phone call from Patrick's assistant, Barbara, telling me that she had a friend who had a friend, Gill, who had MS and could she put her in touch with me? I told her that she was very welcome to do so and we arranged a lunch where we could meet. The day of the lunch came around and I went to the restaurant feeling apprehensive about telling another MSer about my treatment for the first time. "What if I'm wrong?" I thought, "What if I'm setting up false hope for other people?" I was also scared that the treatment might do people harm.

I arrived at the restaurant first and after a few minutes Barbara turned up with her friend, Paul, and Gill. I was aware that Gill was likely to be apprehensive as well so I tried to put her at her ease straight away. It transpired that Paul, who was paying for the lunch, was a friend of Gill's husband Bill. He and Barbara were not going to stay for lunch but Paul ordered a bottle of champagne so they could have a drink with us before they left. Within minutes of meeting her I asked Gill how the MS was affecting her. She told me that she had pain in her hip which made walking difficult, she suffered from fatigue which meant she had to take a nap every afternoon and that her arms were weak to the point where she had trouble dressing herself. Gill was forty-nine years old and had been diagnosed in 1975. To put her at her ease I said "Do you have problems with bladder incontinence as well?" She immediately admitted that she did indeed have problems with urgency and frequency. I then told her the story of the bowel incontinence and having to cut myself out of my jeans. Gill and I ended up giggling to each other as people with MS have a tendency to do when swopping stories. Paul and Barbara were obviously feeling uncomfortable with the conversation and made their excuses to leave. Gill and I waved them away airily and carried on talking. We sat there having lunch and drinking far too much alcohol and talking for seven hours! The next day a courier arrived at my office with a parcel for me. Somewhat perplexed I opened the bag and found a bottle of champagne and a note from Gill. In her letter she had written that she was grateful to me for meeting her and telling her about that treatment and, no matter what the outcome was, she would always be grateful to me for giving her hope. I made a promise to myself that day that I wouldn't open the champagne until I secured a deal with a pharmaceutical company.

Gill went to her GP to ask for the drugs but they refused to take it seriously. She was distressed that her only chance of recovery, as far as she was concerned, had been denied her. Gill rang me to ask what she could do to get hold of the drugs in order to try the treatment in the hope that, if she could show her GP that it worked, then they would prescribe for her. I thought long and hard about what Gill could do and what, ethically, I could do to help. I finally told her that I would give her a two-week supply of my drugs so that she could get started. I reckoned that if she was going to show improvement then she would see it within two weeks. Gill and her husband, Bill, and I met again for lunch and I handed over the pills. They were both inordinately grateful if a little scared to hope that the treatment might work for Gill. Gill started taking her pills the next morning as I had instructed her to do. Four days after she began my treatment I rang Gill to see how she was getting on. I was initially concerned when I heard Gill's voice as she sounded strange, not her normal bubbly self. "How are you feeling?" I asked. "Oh Cari," she said "I don't know what to say." She then went on to explain that all her MS symptoms had gone! She no longer had any pain and the fatigue was clear and her arms were back to normal strength. She told me about how she had gone shopping the day before and had carried two heavy bags back without having to stop for a rest. Gill explained that, previously, when she got back from shopping, she had to sit down for several minutes to recover

before she could unpack the bags. This time she had walked all
the way back from the shops, unpacked the bags and wondered
what to do next, so she went into the garden to prune the roses!
"I hate you Cari!" she said down the 'phone. "Why's that?" I
asked smiling to myself, I guessed what was coming. "I have so
much energy" Gill replied "And I can't remember what I used to
do with a whole day!" I told Gill that I was delighted for her but
not to get too carried away with overdoing things and tiring
herself out. I reminded her that we still had MS and must still
take care of ourselves. "Stuff that," Gill replied "This is
brilliant." As Gill had been in remission for nearly ten years she
was able to benefit from the treatment without having the B12
injections which are only required when the MS is in an active
phase. And so I had the first piece of evidence that my treatment
wasn't a fluke, although, as my father pointed out, "One swallow
does not make a summer".

Gill had two distant relatives with MS, Esther and John, who
in due course rang me to ask about the treatment. I dealt with
them over the phone, taking down their case histories and
making as sure as I could that it would be safe for them to try the
treatment. This in essence meant making sure that they didn't
have any heart problems or high blood pressure. All I could do
was check things like that out and make sure they drew it to
the attention of the GPs when they saw them. Esther reported
that her balance was poor, both legs were weak and that she was
in constant pain. She started the treatment on 4 March and six
days later she rang to tell me that, as far as she was concerned,
her level of disability had reversed to what it had been a year ago.
Her balance was better, she was in less pain, her legs were less
spastic and were about fifty per cent stronger. As a consequence
her mobility was much improved.

John, who was forty-two, was diagnosed twelve years ago and had chronic progressive MS. He was using a wheelchair all the time, his speech was badly affected and he was virtually blind. His hands and head shook uncontrollably and he was, therefore, unable to feed himself. He was also doubly incontinent. As John was unable to speak clearly, Sally his wife, had been dealing with me on his behalf. John started on the treatment while he and Sally were on holiday in Portugal. When they returned home Sally rang me to tell me that the treatment was pure magic. After five days John had started speaking clearly enough to be understood, and, as his hands and head were shaking much less, he could hold a cup steadily enough to drink from without assistance.

I now had four of us on the treatment and showing improvement so, to keep the drug company happy, I only needed one more. Carolyn came to me via a relative of hers who was a colleague of mine at work. She was forty-one and had been diagnosed with remitting-relapsing MS in 1981. Her legs were weak and her balance was poor so she had been using crutches to walk since November 1994. She told me that her right hand was numb and that arm was uncoordinated. The fatigue was so bad that she had to sleep for a while every afternoon. Carolyn started on my treatment on 11 April and rang me on the 14th to tell me that she had stopped using crutches, and now she only needed a stick to walk and could go upstairs normally. She also reported that she no longer had to sleep in the afternoon. Carolyn was so excited about her recovery that she got carried away one day and decided to walk downstairs without holding on to the banister. As a result one of her knees gave way and she fell, tearing the ligaments in her knee. She rang me up to tell me about her accident, which incidentally had happened on her birthday, and said she felt incredibly stupid. "Yup," I said. "That was a pretty daft thing to have done. Have you learned your lesson now?" The problem was that when people started to recover from the MS they acted like kids in a sweetshop for the first time, they wanted everything *now*. I understood as I had reacted exactly the same way.

I sent all the information about the people on my trial to the drug company who had set me the challenge and was convinced that they would have no choice but to take the patent on the basis of my evidence. A few days later I received a letter from Steve at the drug company saying that he was sorry but the director of the Neurochemistry unit felt that the patent was not worth taking as my evidence was only anecdotal and therefore worthless. Steve told me that the director did not want to take on any more work and had thought he was setting me an unachievable goal which, when I delivered it, annoyed him and he had to come up with another reason for the company not to take my patent. I was deeply disappointed and extremely annoyed with the company whom I felt had been stringing me along.

The word had got out at work about my treatment and people who had friends or family with MS started to ask me if they could put them in touch with me. I told them that I didn't mind and would happily talk to them if they wanted to ring me. The partner of one of my colleagues, Jenny, was the editor of a professional science newspaper called *Laboratory News*. Jenny had told him about my breakthrough and he had asked her to tell me that he would be very interested in running the story. I was put in touch with an editor, Charlotte, from the paper and we met one lunchtime. She was fascinated by the story and was very keen to write an article about it. I explained to her that she could not reveal what the drugs were but, other than that, she could write what she wanted. I knew exactly what would happen when the article was printed. I would get bombarded by people wanting to know what the treatment was and wanting to go on it. However, I had exhausted my list of the big drug companies and had drawn a blank so I knew I had to get the information in front of some of the smaller ones in the hope that they might be interested. I thought getting an article in *Laboratory News* was an easy way to achieve that.

The paper with the article in it was published at the beginning of May. The title of the article was "Challenging Current Thinking on MS". I waited for the phones to start ringing. I didn't have to wait long as at nine o'clock in the morning the day after the paper was released my work phone rang. "I have just read an article in *Laboratory News* which talks about your new MS treatment," a man said. "Oh yes," I replied, and waited. "I was very interested," the man said, "as my wife has MS and I wondered if there was any way she could find out more about the treatment." I told him to get her to ring me and I would deal with her. From then on my phone never stopped ringing. As soon as I picked it up I could hear a bleep in the background telling me that another call was waiting, and as soon as I hung up it would ring again. On that first day the Institute switchboard was jammed for six hours with people trying to get through to me. This went on from nine o'clock in the morning to the time I left the office at about half past six in the evening, from Monday to Friday for three weeks.

Before I knew it, I had over one hundred people on my computer database that I had had to set up in order to keep track of everyone. I was completely exhausted after the first two weeks of dealing with the phone calls and simply could not see how I could continue. I was spending anything up to forty minutes talking to every person who rang in order to screen them. Most of them wanted to tell me their complete stories from the time they first felt something was wrong, through being diagnosed and up to the present day. Many of them were highly emotional, several had appalling problems speaking and more than a few ended up in tears. In essence I ended up counselling many of them. By the end of the third week I knew that I had to close down on the trial for the sake of my own health and sanity. All my life consisted of was dealing with phone calls all day, going home and falling asleep without even bothering to have dinner. I was also supposed to be holding down a full-time job at the Institute.

I was deeply affected by the people who rang me. So many of them were too scared to dare hope that they might be able to get better. They had lived so long without hope, some of them for longer than I had been alive. When one of them would start to get emotional when I was telling them about how the treatment worked and what it might be able to do for them, I would say "Hope is hell isn't it?" That normally reduced them to tears. I would tell them that most people felt like they did, that it was OK to feel scared. I did my best to comfort them and would talk them through the way they were feeling, explaining that it had been easy for me because I had had no expectations until I recovered, whereas they knew what might happen to them. I urged them to discuss their feelings with their partners who would probably be feeling just as scared to hope. Whenever I put down the phone after someone had been crying I felt emotionally drained. Doubts haunted me. I was still unable truly to believe that I had developed a new treatment that actually worked. I lived with the constant belief that, sooner or later, someone would see through the bluff, that I would be held up to public ridicule as a liar and a quack. It was only when the seventh person on my trial reported in to say that they were seeing improvement that I finally believed that what I was doing was for real. It wasn't simply the realisation that my treatment worked for other people and all the implications that held, but, most importantly, that my own health was now safe for the foreseeable future. I felt that I should do something to mark that day so I went to Oxford Street with the intention of buying a keepsake. I ended up buying a diamond and sapphire ring that had seven stones in it, three sapphires and four clusters of diamonds. "Seven stones to mark seven people," I thought. "And diamonds are supposed to be for ever." I wore that ring every day from then on and each time I looked at it I remembered that auspicious day.

Every person on my trial had their own special story of battling against adversity, fighting the difficulties of increasing disability, having the possibility of an independent life taken away from them, dealing with the response of society, but also of sharing the love and happiness of their spouses and children. I consider it an immense privilege that all the people who contacted me shared their stories with me and trusted me enough to bother to try to get the drugs from their doctors. I believe that, had I been them, I would have laughed at what people were telling me, perhaps not even bothered to pick up the phone and ring. Why on earth should anyone take "happy pills and cola" seriously as a treatment for MS?

Once people started finding their way to me and got the drugs from their doctors and, subsequently, started to show improvement, I asked them why they ever believed me. Their responses took me aback. They told me that firstly I was a person with MS

and, therefore, as far as they were concerned I would not lie to
them as I knew first-hand the pain that false hope can cause. The
second thing that apparently convinced them was that I was not
selling anything. I was not asking them to pay for the
information or to pay me for the drugs. In other words I was not
trying to make a fast buck. As far as I was concerned, I had got
my life back against the odds and it was only ethical to offer
fellow sufferers the same chance.

John is a forty-five-year-old father of seven-year-old triplets.
He was diagnosed with MS in 1983 and by the time he found his
way to me was using a wheelchair at least half of the time. His
legs were spastic and weak, as were his arms. He, in common
with many MS sufferers, had to cope with bladder urgency and
occasional incontinence. His speech had a tendency to become
slightly slurred when he became tired. The MS fatigue was ever
present, further preventing him from participating in the full
chaotic lives of his children. He was the fourth person ever to
find their way to me as a result of knowing someone who had
heard about my treatment. When John first contacted me I took
down, as I had to for every person contacting me about the trial,
the details about when he was first diagnosed, what his
symptoms were at the time of phoning and any drugs he was
taking for symptomatic relief. I also checked to make sure he had
no history of heart problems, which is the only thing that could
really make the treatment dangerous.

John finally got the drugs from his GP and started the
treatment on April Fools' Day! Four days later I received a call
from John telling me that his level of fatigue was much less, his
hands were subjectively less numb, his arms stronger, his speech
was clear all the time, the spasticity in his legs was better and
they were stronger, and the bladder incontinence was greatly

improved. John is now increasingly using grab bars and crutches to walk more of the time.

Towards the end of April John asked me to go and have Sunday afternoon tea with his family as we had never met before. After I had been there for a while one of his triplets came up to me and started to ask questions. She looked at me rather quizzically and said, "Do you have MS like daddy?" I told her that indeed I did. She chewed her lip for a moment and then asked, "Is it your treatment that daddy is on?" I explained to her that, yes, I was taking the same treatment as him. She pondered this for a moment longer and then said, with a certain amount of anxiety in her voice, "Will daddy get better like you?" I nodded but told her that it might take until she was about nine years old. In other words it was not going to happen overnight. She then ran across the patio and flung herself into my arms and hugged me tightly. Finally she looked up at me grinning from ear to ear and told me that she could see that her daddy was already getting better and that she couldn't wait until he could play football with her! It was moments like this that made me begin to realise the true enormity of what I had discovered. The treatment was not only changing the lives of people with MS but those of their families and friends as well.

Imran is a twenty-eight-year-old man who was diagnosed with remitting-relapsing MS at the age of twenty-two. At the time of my taking down his details he was having to use a stick to walk as his legs were very weak and he also suffered from tremors and muscle spasms in them. He had problems with bladder urgency and frequency and, as a result, had to get up two or three times during the night to go to the bathroom. His arms were weak and he had problems with the coordination of his left arm. Fatigue was a real problem. He had to have a sleep in the afternoons in order to get through the day. When he got tired his speech became slow and slurred and he often became short of breath. He was experiencing problems with his short-term memory which, as he was studying for a PhD, was a real handicap. As a result of having to deal with the disabilities and the knowledge that it was only likely to get worse as the years wore on, he felt that he had little hope of living an independent life, having a wife and family, or a career.

Imran had heard about Beta Interferon, the much-heralded treatment that had found its way across from the States and had been using Rebif for six months prior to hearing about my treatment. He was also taking a drug, Oxybutanin, to help with bladder control. I explained to Imran that, if he felt that the Rebif was helping him, then I would advise him to stay on it but if he wanted to try my treatment then he must stop using Rebif as the possible interactions could not be predicted and may indeed (for all I knew) be dangerous. As the Beta Interferons can only, at best, slow down the progression of the disease whereas my treatment was actually reversing disability, Imran felt that he wanted to go for mine. After a brief battle with his GP he started on the treatment on 7 June. Five days later he rang to tell me that he no longer suffered from fatigue and was walking from time to time without a stick as his legs were stronger and were shaking much less dramatically. His bladder control was so much better that he had given up taking Oxybutanin and very rarely had to get up in the night to go to the bathroom. He also reported that his speech was clear even when he was tired and that his breathing was much less laboured. His arms were stronger and the coordination in the left arm was better.

Imran was one of the few people who decided from the start to keep a daily diary in order to chart his progress. He sent me a copy of his diary every ten days which, I think, gives a wonderful insight into what the treatment has done for him.

Imran's diary August 1995: The month got off to a flying start with my visit to my neurologist. The success of this visit was supported by my appointment at the physio's. The weather is still unusually hot—trust the summer to be the hottest on record for 250 years. After experimenting with my cold baths, which has included staying in for longer, I have settled on twenty minutes followed by a cold shower and then my exercises. I realise that while the summer is with us I must do all my jobs in the morning. Eating whatever takes my fancy is never a problem any more. Although the weather is still hot and disguises the improvements, I am confident that this combinations of drugs is working.

On the 2nd of August I had my six-monthly visit to my neurologist. He was impressed by my walking, albeit with the aid of a stick. He was even more impressed once I had told him that I was no longer taking Beta-Interferon. His amazement was not to stop here. After giving me the routine neurological tests he concluded that I was certainly a lot stronger all over. It was only at the end that I told him that I had been taking this "magical remedy". The other successes I have to report since my last diary include: picking up and walking with my baby niece; and most importantly, buying a house. Regarding the last subject, I have been able to go shopping for sofas, paints, tiles etc. I can also report that since my last diary my mood has been good and positive. I know the drugs are working and that is why I feel confident about the future.

To the amazement of my family I walked on the grass in the garden without the aid of my stick. Instead I used my stick as a

*golf club with which to practise my swing. I no longer religiously
watch my diet, which is a wonderful improvement to my quality
of life. I also decided to swim today. The swimming went well—
I even did back-stroke for the first time for a few years. After
lunch with a friend, who hadn't seen me for a few weeks, they
remarked that I looked alive. God knows what I must have
looked like before!*

*Last week I went away to Scotland for a short break which
was brilliant. I had always dreamt about sitting on the beach and
reading: this dream became a reality, as I sat on the beach for at
least five hours not worrying about the sun or needing the toilet*

*The weather has certainly worked against me, but I now
seem to know what my limitations are and what I must do to
keep cool. When I have wanted ice-cream or any other junk
food, I have indulged without feeling guilty. I know myself that I
feel positive about the future which buying a house illustrates.*

The change in the way Imran talked when he rang me up and
the things he started to talk about being able to do, or that he
was planning for his future, consistently delighted me. Every
time he rang me up to tell me what he could do as a result of the
treatment I was left rocking and reeling with incredulity.

Sarah is forty-four years old and has been battling against MS
since the age of seventeen. When she found her way to me she
was walking with two sticks indoors with great difficulty but had
to use an electric scooter outside. Her legs were very spastic,
weak and painful, and she experienced muscle spasms in both
legs. Her hands were so weak that she was unable to cut up her
own food which she had to rely on her partner to do for her. She
suffered badly from fatigue and her balance was poor.

Sarah started on my treatment on 15 June and after five days reported that she was walking better with her sticks indoors, that the fatigue was clear, her ability to write had improved and that she could wiggle toes for the first time in years! After a couple more weeks she rang to share the news with me that she could once again eat with cutlery and cut up her own food for the first time in one and a half years and that her coordination was better. Sarah regularly went to have physiotherapy and was thrilled when her therapist spontaneously commented on how much better she was walking and performing her exercises.

The highlight for me came when I spoke to Sarah nine weeks after she started on my treatment. I was just ringing her to see how she was getting on as I did periodically with all the people on my trial. I was stunned by the news that the day before she had managed to walk thirty-five yards outside, while holding on to a friend's arm, which she reported was the farthest she had been able to walk for two years. I was so happy for her that I would have hugged her if she had not been on the other end of the 'phone. The news did not stop there though. She told me that she was going to start using crutches in a few days time on the urging of her physiotherapist. A week after that piece of news, Sarah rang me again on a Sunday afternoon saying that she simply had to ring because she was so excited. She had just come back from the gym and her instructor had been absolutely thrilled at how strong she was and how well she could do all the exercises compared to a few weeks ago. But the *coup de grâce* was that she could now walk 100 yards holding on to a friend's arm!

One day I received a phone call from Nicky the full-time live-in carer of sixty-three-year-old Neil who had been diagnosed with chronic progressive MS in 1972. Nicky started off by telling me that she feared that Neil, or the "governor" as she called him, was probably too far gone to be helped but that he had nothing left to lose by trying *anything* now. However, by this time I had dealt with some pretty severely affected people and had been getting very positive reports back on how they were doing. So I told Nicky that, as far I could ascertain, it was never too late for this treatment to benefit the person with MS.

Nicky told me that Neil had been using an electric wheel-chair 100% of the time for the past five years. Both his legs were badly spastic and the muscles severely wasted. He suffered from muscle spasms in both legs which caused him quite a lot of pain. He had little or no movement at all in either his arms or legs and also suffered from muscle spasms in his arms which were quite painful. He was unable to see anything unless it was virtually in front of his nose. The horrific saga continued as Nicky told me that Neil was unable to speak and had to use an alphabet board to point to letters, with a head pointer, in order to be able to communicate. As if that were not enough for any one person to have to cope with, he had lost both his cough and gag reflexes which often leads to pneumonia as a result of inhaling food or liquid. Pneumonia is the most common cause of premature death in people with MS. In order to prevent him developing pneumonia again he had not been allowed to eat or drink for eighteen months and was fed through a tube in his stomach. Neil was living my own personal nightmare and I was desperate to help him.

Neil, like Imran, had been taking Beta Interferon for six months but had already decided to give up on that as it made him feel so unwell. He was also having to take Tegretol to help with the pain, Baclofen for spasticity, and Diazepam (a tranquilliser) at night to try and help him sleep which he had a lot of trouble with.

Neil started the treatment on 1 July and on the 3rd I received a call from a totally gobsmacked Nicky. She initially worried me to death by telling me that Neil had started crying that morning when she was getting him up out of bed. I began to panic, thinking that the treatment had made him feel even worse. She finally told me that, after she asked him why he was crying, he managed to explain to her that, for the first time in two years, he could see the pictures on the wall the other side of his bedroom! His sight was coming back after only two days on the treatment. He was so overwhelmed that the only emotional response he was capable of was to cry. During the next week Nicky rang to tell me that Neil was beginning to speak and that his speech was getting stronger and clearer by the day. Also that the muscle spasms were better, that he was sitting up straighter in his wheelchair as his back and stomach muscles got stronger, that he was sleeping better at night, that he could move his right arm enough to scratch his nose when it itched, could now give people the thumbs-up, and that his fatigue was gone.

On 11 July she rang to tell me that Neil's speech therapist had been out to see him and was very impressed by the fact that his gag and cough reflexes were back. She asked Nicky if there was any ice cream in the house and immediately got Neil to eat some while she watched. She confirmed that Neil could eat a little ice cream or jelly each day to get him used to eating again. This was the first time that anything had passed Neil's lips in eighteen months.

Two months after he started on my treatment I received a card from Imran in which he had written "I would just like to thank you for, as the MS Society would say, giving me a hope in hell!" Imran was referring to the MS Society's by-line "The MS Society. A hope in hell". For me this sums up how the people improving on my treatment seem to feel about the way it has changed their lives.

I cannot begin to explain how I felt when people like Sarah, Imran, John and Neil (via Nicky) reported in to tell me how they were improving. I felt so responsible for each and every one of them that I was terrified in case the treatment did not work for them and their hopes and dreams would be shattered once again. Every time a person on my trial rang in for the first time to tell me that they were getting better I was not only thrilled for them but I privately breathed a sigh of relief. I found it hard to believe that I had inadvertently found a solution to this living hell and, from time to time, I would go through a crisis of confidence. I had met with extreme scepticism from the MS Society and from their Research Advisory Board which is comprised of neurologists, and on occasion, when I was exhausted and worn down, I began to think that they must be right and I had got it all wrong. But then another person on my trial would ring in for the first time telling me that they could now see better, or walk better or talk better and I would know, all over again, that I must not give up. I would realise that the treatment was too important to let sceptics stand in the way of getting it through to proper clinical trials.

At that time I felt incredibly alone. It felt as if I was the only person prepared to put their neck on the line as far as battling to get the medical profession to look at the treatment seriously was concerned. But I was also painfully aware that hundreds of thousands of people with MS were placing their hopes on me and I felt that I owed it to every single one of them to carry on fighting.

Once I had closed down on the trial I had to deal with the guilt of telling people who rang me for the first time, having heard about my treatment, that I wasn't able to take on any more people. I tried to be as gentle as I could in imparting the news but the disappointment in their voices was hard to take. Virtually everyone was very understanding and said things like, "Well, I've waited fifteen years I guess a few more won't hurt" and they all wished me luck. On the other hand I had one man who was so incensed that I wouldn't tell him what the drugs were that he swore at me and told me that I was the most evil bitch he had ever encountered. "I can't believe what I'm hearing," he yelled. "You have the answer to my living hell and you don't give a shit about me." I explained to him that I was doing everything in my power to get the treatment out for everyone as quickly as possible but he would not listen. He kept asking why I couldn't just tell him and I explained that I had to screen everyone first to make sure that they could safely use the treatment. "You don't have to" he yelled "Just tell me the fucking drugs". I asked him if he thought it would be ethical for me to tell him the drugs if it might kill him, to which he responded "Well you aren't dead . . . so stop fucking me about". He made me feel incredibly guilty. I was nearly in tears by the time I put the phone down. I had tried to explain to him that if I dealt with just one more person then, morally, I would have to deal with everyone and I simply couldn't cope as the calls were coming through at the rate of about twenty a day. I was racked with guilt over having to turn people away. How could I deny anyone the chance of getting their lives back the way I and many others had? I had to keep reminding myself that there were 80,000 people in the UK with MS but that there was only one of me.

Every other day or so someone would ring up and their story would tug at my heartstrings. Mothers would ring me up to tell me that their twenty-year-old son was virtually paralysed by MS, or a husband would explain that his wife was bedbound and that they had two young children, or a person my age with MS would call me who had a friend who was on my trial and had seen how they had recovered. It was those cases that I gave in to. I knew that I could help those people and my conscience would not allow me to turn them away. They needed help and they needed it now, not later. They were all inordinately grateful to be taken on as "special cases". I told everyone that there were no guarantees although it was worth a try, but they all believed in me so unequivocally that they said "I trust you. I know this is the answer." Once again I felt under enormous pressure from people's expectations. What would they think of me if the treatment didn't work for them?

There were a few people who didn't seem to respond the way the others had but in nearly every case I managed to work out what had gone wrong. In several cases it was as simple as the fact that they had bought the wrong brand of amino acid (contrary to my instructions), or were taking their anti-depressant at night instead of in the morning as I had told them to. I must admit that I began to have immense empathy with doctors for the first time in my life. I knew exactly what they meant when they talked about patient non-compliance! I also realised how specialists could get dismissive of people's complaints so easily. By the time that I had dealt with close to 200 people, all with the same illness, I pretty much knew what each was going to tell me. I developed a style of screening them which meant that I would run through the normal symptoms and ask if they suffered from them. "How are the legs?" I would ask and enter their response on my database. "Are your legs spastic? Are the muscles tight? Do you get muscle spasms? And how about bladder control? Urgency and frequency?" I would work from the legs upwards until I had covered the whole body and then I would ask them if they had any problems that I hadn't asked about. "I think you have covered the lot!" they would normally reply. Many of them commented that I had asked about problems that their neurologist had never bothered to mention. I guess that was because I had MS myself.

One of the more difficult cases I had to deal with was a young mother, Pauline. She had been on the treatment for about five weeks and had seen no improvement. She rang me up to tell me that nothing was happening and to ask me if there was anything she could do. I checked that she had got the correct amino acid, that she was taking the drugs at the right time and that she wasn't taking any other prescription drugs or supplements. I asked her how much she weighed as I knew that if people were twelve stone or more they had to take a higher dose of the drugs. "Oh no," she said. "I am seven and a half stone." She paused and then said, "I have lost a lot of weight recently though." That alerted me so I asked her how much she had lost and in what space of time. It transpired that she had lost three stone in the last year. "What does your GP have to say about that?" I asked. "He says I am just depressed," she replied. I continued to probe and finally got it out of her that the weight loss had started as soon as she was diagnosed with MS. The alarm bells had started to ring in my head. "Are you eating?" I asked. She told me that she had breakfast. "Is that all? You mean you don't eat for the rest of the day?" I said. "Not really," she replied in a miserable voice. I asked her what she had for breakfast and she told me that she ate grapes. "Shit girl!" I yelped down the phone. "You're starving yourself to death. Don't you realise how important it is to eat? Especially with MS" There was no response and I suddenly realised she was sobbing uncontrollably. "Sweetheart, are you anorexic?" I said gently. Pauline was barely capable of talking as she was crying so hard but she finally choked out,

162

"Yes." I asked her if she had ever told anyone else and she admitted she hadn't. Having been bulimic myself for the previous ten years I knew just what she was going through right then. I understood how frightening it was to admit to someone that you were hiding such a deep, dark secret. I talked to her gently, trying to calm her down. I got her to explain to me how she coped with preparing meals for her husband and child and how they reacted to her sitting at the table not eating. Although Pauline was in a wheelchair, her husband expected her to function exactly as she had before getting MS. He gave her no help at all. Her relatives and friends had also abandoned her as they didn't want to have to deal with the reality of MS.

My heart went out to Pauline, no one should have to live the way she was. I told her that she was immensely brave to have told me about her anorexia and offered to put her in touch with the Eating Disorders Association which she said she would like to do. I also asked her if she would like talk to someone on the MS Society helpline who could give her information about getting a home help to give her assistance with shopping and preparing meals. Pauline had the additional difficulty that she was unable to write so she couldn't take down the phone numbers so I suggested that I contact the helpline and get them to ring her. I said I would arrange that and that I would ring her later that afternoon to see how she was feeling. After about an hour and a half I put the phone down and sat there with my head in my hands, feeling numb. The fact was that Pauline's metabolism had closed down due to not eating and that was probably responsible for the treatment not working. I rang Pauline later that afternoon and was surprised when she said that she couldn't talk as she had a friend with her.

Two days later Pauline rang me back again to tell me that

treatment was working. "Are you eating?" I asked. "I had lunch the day I spoke to you," she said, "and I am eating proper meals with the family now." I asked her why she had suddenly been able to eat, to which she replied, "You told me that I couldn't get better if I didn't, so I decided to eat." I think that episode overwhelmed me almost more than any other. Every so often I would think, "What the hell am I doing? I'm not a scientist or a medic or a counsellor!" I felt bound by the medic's edict, "First do no harm", but I was still haunted by fears about whether potentially I could damage anyone. Whether the treatment harmed me down the line was, as far as I was concerned, irrelevant. I had decided right from the start that if I had five or six normal productive years and then dropped dead as a result of the treatment I would be perfectly happy.

The other thing I found myself dealing with was coping with the spouse of the person with MS. Gill's husband Bill was the first. Shortly after Gill made her miraculous recovery Bill rang me to ask he could have lunch with me as he needed to talk. I assumed he wanted to tell me how well Gill was doing and how happy he was and consequently was dumbfounded when he told me that he was finding it quite difficult to cope with. It transpired that Bill had been performing the role of not only a husband but Gill's carer as well for many years. He had to do the shopping and cooking and dress her when she got up and help her to go to bed. He had got used to the lifestyle and to the fact that they no longer had an active sex life due to Gill's exhaustion. Suddenly, out of the blue, Bill had his wife back again. Gill was racing around and doing all the things that Bill had previously been doing for her. His role had been taken away from him. He was also finding it quite hard to keep up with her! He related one story to me which, I have to admit, I had a hard time not laughing at. "We were going to bed one night," Bill said "And I was sitting on the bed waiting for Gill to come out of the bathroom so I could help her undress and get into bed." I nodded and waited, having a sneaky suspicion what was coming next. "She appeared in the bedroom door wearing her best black lacy underwear" said Bill "And asked me if I was in the mood for it!" I tried my hardest not to laugh but couldn't help but grin. "And?" I asked. "Well," said Bill "It had been a long time since we had done anything like that!". We both started to laugh at that point. I understood then how he must be feeling. Bill and I talked about the effect on the spouses of people who were recovering and he offered to talk to the partners if any of them were encountering the same feelings as he was. He had gone through feeling guilty about not being overtly happy for Gill to start with. Partly it was that he felt he needed to keep his feet on the ground in case the treatment failed and Gill would need him to be strong enough to cope with her disappointment, and partly that his life had been changed.

From then on I warned people that their spouses might not be as overtly happy as they would expect them to be, but that they must talk it through and give them time to get used to the changes. "Your recovery is almost as big as a shock for you and your partner as getting MS was in the first place," I would tell people, and it was true. They both brought about major changes in people's lives. I know that for me on 19 August 1994 the MS symptoms going away was indeed almost as big a shock, albeit a wonderful one, as waking up with MS in October 1992 had been.

I heard the shock in people's voices when they rang up to tell me that they were getting better, or in the case of five people, that their symptoms had completely gone in the space of two or three days. Maybe shock isn't the right word but there was certainly a sense of wonderment in the way they spoke. One afternoon I got a phone call on my mobile (which I had got to try and take the pressure off me) from a lady, Denni, who had started on the treatment only two days before. "Hi Denni," I said. "How's it going sweetheart?" "I had to ring you," she said in a tearful voice. "When we first spoke you gave me hope that there was light at the end of the tunnel. I'm ringing to tell you that I'm out of the tunnel and standing in the sunshine." Her words sent shivers down my spine. I had never had anyone express, quite so eloquently, the way they felt. It transpired that after having lived with some level of disability for twenty-one years since she was diagnosed at the age of twenty, Denni had gone a hundred per cent clear in forty-eight hours on the treatment. Six little tablets was all it took. "Cari, do you realise what you have done?" Denni asked me. "You have done it. You have got the answer to this evil disease. You have really done it girl!" I think we were both nearly in tears by then. It was the first time that anyone had said that to me. I asked Denni how she was going to celebrate but she had no idea how to cope with the magnitude and speed of her recovery. I gave her strict instructions that she had to go out to dinner that night and drink lots of booze and toast her recovery! "Celebrate!" I said. "Believe me, I know how important that is to make it seem real."

✦

CHAPTER SEVEN

FLYING HIGH

✦

IF I was under the impression that my life had changed up to that point, then I was in for a shock. In May 1995 things started to speed up. As a result of the *Laboratory News* article I had been approached by a pharmaceutical company who wanted to take a licence on my patent in order to develop the treatment and put it on the market. As I am sure you can imagine I was terribly excited at the prospect but I realised that if this was indeed going to happen then I would need a financial adviser and an accountant. I vaguely remembered seeing something in an Institute of Education staff handbook about personal financial advice for members of staff. I trawled through the drawers in my office and finally found the handbook I was looking for. I flicked through it and, sure enough, there was a note about the fact that the Institute had an agreement with a financial firm who would provide advice on personal finance free of charge. "What have I got to lose?" I thought, and picked up the phone to ring them. I was assuming that they would only give free advice on things like pensions, so when I got the contact man, David, on the line I opened the conversation by saying, "This probably isn't the kind of request you get very often from a member of Institute staff." I went on to explain the situation I was facing and what I might be needing in terms of advice fairly soon. David wasn't in the least bit fazed and arranged to come to my office to meet me the next day. He arrived and almost immediately asked me to tell him the story of the treatment breakthrough. When I had run through it as briefly as I could he sat there with a look of complete amazement on his face (an expression that I was going to get used to over the next few months). He explained what he could do for me and then said "The first thing you have got to have, though, is an accountant." I told him that I was aware of that but that I had no idea how to go about identifying a good one. David told me that he would sort it out for me and get back to me the next day. He was as good as his word, calling me the next morning to tell me that he had spoken to the accountant that his firm used who had said that he would be happy to meet me. A few days later David turned up at my office with the accountant, Nigel. Once again I had to tell the story for Nigel's benefit and his reaction was almost the same as David's. They were so excited about the prospect of a cure for MS that they just wanted to be associated with what I was doing and give me as much help as they could. So I now had a patent agent, a financial adviser and an accountant. "Blimey," I thought. "I'm turning into Cari Loder plc!". My "advisers" were incredibly helpful to me in professional terms as well as becoming good friends who gave me all the support and encouragement I could have hoped for.

On 21 July I went back to see Dr O'Connor as arranged. I walked through the door to the consulting room and he greeted me by saying "Hello, how are you then? Still bouncing, I assume?" He checked out my walking and balance and reflexes and asked to see me run up and down the stairs in the teaching room. He couldn't wipe the grin off his face as, test after test, he found no neurological signs. He finally told me that he would write to Ray and that he would see me again in six months. "You *are* going to tell him that I am one hundred per cent clear aren't you?" I asked. "OK," he replied. "I guess I can this time." I whooped with glee and said "Heh, you're going to start seeing me once a year before long aren't you?" "Of course," Dr O'Connor replied, so I told him that I would miss him. He grinned at me and said, "Yes. I thought you might." He then asked me to make an early appointment in the clinic the next time I saw him so that I was there before the students left. "They like seeing you," he commented. So there it was. Less than three years from the time I was diagnosed of MS I had received the all-clear.

I had been communicating with a pharmaceutical company, Scotia, for a couple of weeks. On Monday 31 July my phone rang and it was David from Scotia. He had read my patent statement before he went abroad and remembered it well. We spoke for a while about how my trial was going and I finally said, "Do you think that Scotia might, possibly, be interested in taking the patent, in some form or another?" I held my breath, expecting the normal let down. David chuckled and said, "If you are asking me if I want it then the answer is yes." "Really?" I squeaked. "Of course," he said "This is terribly exciting." He then said "How do you feel about double blind placebo clinical trials?" to which I replied, "What do you mean? We have no choice if we want this to be taken seriously by the medical profession." "Good,"

David said. "Most inventors drop it at that point because they want their treatment made available immediately." "No way," I responded. "The name of the game right now is slow but sure and nail it at every step." David then asked me if I would draft a protocol for the trials and let him have it as soon as I could. "Umm . . . OK" I said. "But you will remember when you see it that I'm not a scientist or a medic won't you?" "Don't worry," said David. "I am used to dealing with lay researchers." I sat down at my computer and typed up a trial protocol as best I could, complete with predicted outcomes for each group. I faxed it to David immediately, hoping that it wasn't too naive an attempt.

About fifteen minutes later a fax arrived for me from him. It was a copy of an article he had written some years ago called *In Praise of Lay Researchers*. I read it with interest and it became clear why he wasn't fazed by the fact that I wasn't a scientist. At four o'clock that afternoon I received another call from David. "Thank you for your fax," he said. "We're thinking along the same lines. All you need to decide now is what deal you want from us." For a moment I couldn't think straight. I had been battling with drug companies for nine months and getting nowhere and suddenly in the space of a day I had a deal being offered to me. "Good grief!" I said. "Tell you what, David, make me an offer I can't refuse." He chuckled and outlined a deal that they had just done with another inventor to take an exclusive licence on their patent. "That sounds fine to me," I said. "But I will have to talk to my lawyers and accountants about it." "Of course," David said. "And we must meet up. I'll ring you on Wednesday." I hung up and sat there not believing that I had finally done it. After all the battling it didn't seem right that it was so easy at the end. I rang John and Nigel to tell them the news and to alert them to the fact that things were likely to speed up now. David and I failed to make contact on Wednesday but at half past eight in the morning on Thursday I got a call from him to tell me that he was flying to Scotland that morning but would arrive in London late on Friday afternoon and asking if I was free to have dinner with him that evening.

On Friday afternoon I hit a glitch that came out of the blue. I received a call from a writer who had got hold of the information about my treatment from the MS Society. He was writing a book about approaches to treating MS and intended to put my information in it. I explained to him the MS Society had no right to give him the information and that he could not include it in his book. We argued back and forth for a while with me trying to explain to him why he could not use the material and him saying he couldn't see why not. I finally had to tell him that if he were to include my material in his book I would have no choice but to take legal action to prevent the book from being published. David turned up while I was on the phone to my lawyers who were giving me advice on what action I could legitimately take. I waved him in and a few minutes later was able to put the phone down. Before I could say anything, David grinned at me and said, "Cari, I presume. You look like you could do with a drink." I agreed whole-heartedly so I packed up and we left to go to a local restaurant.

I felt very much at ease with David as we walked down the street. He was very down to earth. As it was a hot evening we decided to sit at a table outside the restaurant. We had only just sat down when David said. "Right. I want to hear the whole story." "What?" I asked. "From the time I woke up with MS?" "Sure," he said, "I want to hear it all." I took a deep breath and gave up on the idea of having any chance to eat my meal before it got cold. I worked through my story as quickly as I could without skipping over the essential facts and events. David interrupted from time to time to ask for clarification but otherwise listened while eating his way through the pizza he had ordered. I finally ended my story and took the opportunity to grab a few bites from my meal. "OK," David said. "That was fascinating. Now tell me about you." I looked longingly at my virtually untouched calves' liver and salad and once again launched into the explanation. "So that's me," I said after twenty minutes or so. At last David took over the conversation by telling me about other patents Scotia had taken in the past that had come from non-scientists like me. While he talked I raced through my meal before he had a chance to ask me another question! We chatted about the intricacies of the deal until I was sure that I understood exactly what was being offered. Finally I smiled at David and asked, "Have we got a deal then?" "Sure," he answered and reached over the table to shake hands. So that was it. I had done the deal on giving an exclusive licence on my patent to a drug company less than a year since I had filed it.

Before we parted David told me that he would deal with John, my patent agent, to get an agreement drawn up and that he would also rewrite my patent statement in preparation for international filing. As we were walking back from the restaurant I was mentioning to David the kind of flak I had received from various quarters. "Do you know," I said, "I should be grateful to them in a perverse way. If they hadn't fought me so hard I might not have battled to get the patent taken so quickly." David chuckled and observed that they obviously didn't know me very well and that if they had really wanted to stop me they should have just kept quiet and worked behind the scenes. "I know maverick researchers like you, Cari," he said. "You're all the same. You're trouble." I laughed as he well and truly had me sussed out.

I had been counting down the days during August to the 19th as that would be my one-year anniversary of "going clear" from the MS. As I had observed my one year anniversary of being diagnosed I felt that I *must* celebrate this one. I rang Colm and asked him if he would come out and have dinner with me to help me celebrate. I hadn't realised that my anniversary coincided with the VJ day celebrations until I was about to leave for the restaurant. The weather was still very hot so Colm and I sat at a table outside the same restaurant that I had been to with David. As we were sitting there eating, we started to notice aeroplanes flying over in formation, the most stunning of which was a flight going over forming the number fifty. It all added to the sense of occasion and I was really enjoying myself. Later that evening as it began to get dark, a fireworks display started down on the Thames. We couldn't see the fireworks themselves, but every so often the sky would light up in various colours. I was rather tipsy by then as Colm and I were on our second bottle of champagne, so I got to my feet, raised my glass, and said to the other people sitting outside, "That's all for my celebration you know!" I sat down giggling and feeling rather daft.

On 2 September I had arranged a party for the people on my trial to come and meet me for the first time. The day before the party I had two people ring me up on separate occasions warning me that they had heard that a group of people were threatening to come to the party to cause trouble. These trouble makers would not say who they were or even which part of the country they were from, but let it be known that they intended to "blow the whistle" on my treatment, claiming it didn't work and that I was a liar. I was inordinately upset at the thought of people coming to cause trouble at the party. I didn't care what they threw at me but I hated the thought of them disrupting the party for the people who were coming to celebrate their recovery. I briefed the film crew from the production company who were making a documentary about my story as well as three of my friends, Colm, Charlie and Di. I told them that I intended to flush out the dissenters as quickly as I could at the start of the party and asked them if they would be prepared to try and "ring fence" them for me in order to keep them away from the other people on my trial.

We arrived in the hall at about eleven o'clock while the caterers were setting up the buffet lunch. As the people on my trial had wanted a name for their treatment they had dubbed it "Cari's Cocktail" so I had called the party "Cari's Cocktail" Party. I went round the building putting up posters so people would know where to come when they arrived. I was getting increasingly nervous and had a blinding headache so I wandered around fiddling with my presentation papers and smoking far too much. At a quarter to twelve two men walked through the door to the hall. As I had only ever met three of the people on my trial I had no idea who these people were. "Hello," I said, going over to them. "I'm Cari. Now who are you?" One of the men grinned at me and said, "Don't you recognise the voice?" I racked my brains but having seen him I couldn't focus on his voice. He finally gave in and told me, at which point two more people arrived. I went over to the door to meet them and they too asked me to guess who they were from their voices. I was overwhelmed as people arrived, meeting them for the first time ever. After nine or ten people had come into the hall I saw a lady arrive on her own and walked over to greet her. She stood in the doorway and said gently, "Cari, it's Denni." "Denni!" I shrieked and hugged her. We stood there hugging each other for a long time almost in tears. She finally pulled back, still holding my hands, and said tearfully, "Thank you. Thank you for everything." "Are you really clear of MS now?" I asked her. She nodded and smiled and said, "Look at me. I look like you now. No one would ever know that I had MS." And she was right. We hugged again but I finally had to let her go as more people were arriving.

Suddenly one of the film crew appeared and said that Sarah was just arriving in a taxi at the front of the building. They were very keen to film Sarah getting out of the taxi as the first time they had filmed her she had been unable to walk and had either to be carried or use her scooter. I went out with them as I had never met Sarah before and was desperate to see her. The crew went down to the street where Sarah and her friend were getting out of the taxi but I stood at the top of the steps leading up to the Institute so as to stay out of their way. Sarah had told me that she was walking with crutches now so I watched with interest to see how much more mobile she really was. Suddenly Sarah looked up and saw me. I went down the steps and walked over to her. "Hi sweetheart," I said. "We meet at last." Sarah reached out and hugged me tightly. I pulled back a little to look her in the eyes and saw that she was crying. I hugged her again saying, "Heh, come on. This is supposed to be a happy day", and gently wiped away her tears. She smiled and said "I've wanted to meet you for so long, Cari." I helped her walk as we made our way inside and went down to the hall where the others were waiting. Finally at one o'clock there were about seventy people in the hall talking to one another and sharing their experiences of what the treatment had done for them.

I had decided to make a brief speech to launch the party so I went to the front and stood in front of the microphone. I tapped on it a few times to get everyone's attention and then started speaking. I started by saying, "First of all can I say how wonderful it is to see you all here today. I have got to know many of you well over the telephone over the last few months and it is lovely to finally be able to put faces to names and voices." I looked round the room at so many people that I knew incredibly well from endless conversations on the phone. This was the day that I had been waiting for and it was finally happening. "One thing I have discovered on handling the treatment trial is that everyone has their own special story to tell and I consider it a privilege that so many of you have shared your stories with me." I said. I was beginning to feel rather emotional by then but managed to prevent my voice from cracking.

I continued, "It appears though that we all have two things in common. Firstly of course we all have MS. Secondly, I have never met such a group of people who have maintained their sense of humour *and* their ability to fight against such overwhelming odds. I applaud you all, both MSers and your families and friends." That was greeted with smiles from around the room as many of "my" people had friends or family with them. I then told them about the father of a young man on the treatment who had told me recently about how his son developed MS at the age of twenty-two. He stressed that when you develop MS it is not too strong to say MS strikes. "It is indeed for all of us in one way or another a bolt out of the blue," I said. I then said something that I had wanted to tell all of them for ages "I owe all of you a huge debt of gratitude. You may find that a strange thing for me to say, but were it not for all of you trusting me and trying the treatment I would have not been able to compile the evidence that was needed in order to get this taken seriously by a drug company. I have often wondered what I would have done if I were you and you were me. I know the answer to that. I would have assumed it was another quack idea and would never have even bothered to find out about it. I also want to thank you all for the immense happiness you have brought to my life. Getting your phone calls telling me you are improving and are able to do things that you have not been able to do for maybe years has been a privilege and a joy."

"People have, from time to time, asked me how it feels to have discovered this," I continued, "I will repeat what I said to them. I feel very privileged and incredibly humbled by my role in this." I ended my speech by saying, "Lastly, I hope you will all find a way of saying hello to me before the afternoon ends. There are so many people here today that I have sent hugs down the phone to and I'd really like to be able to deliver at least some of them in person today." People clapped and cheered so I jumped in and yelled, "Let the party begin!"

I was shuffling my papers together when Gill's husband, Bill, came up to me and said "Do you mind if I say something?" "Sure," I replied assuming he meant that he wanted to say something to me, so I was taken aback when he went up to the microphone and started speaking. Bill spoke about how Gill had been for years before the treatment and how she was now. "I have got my wife back," he said, "and the children have their mother again." Bill continued speaking about how much Gill and he owed me and my magic treatment and how we had first met and the support and encouragement I had given them. I was finding it overwhelming to hear someone speak about me in those terms and when Bill finished speaking and came over to me I was nearly in tears. He stood in front of me, took my hands and said with an emotional smile, "I meant every word Cari. You're wonderful." I burst into tears and hugged him for what felt like ages until I got myself under control again. For just a couple of minutes I had not been able to duck the reality of what I had done. All the time since I had discovered the treatment I had brushed off what I had done saying "I didn't do anything really. It was all a fluke." I felt that if I consciously acknowledged the reality of what I had done I would go mad. It was just too huge to get my head around, but hearing what Bill said I had no choice but to believe it for the first time, although five minutes later I was laughing it off again. During the course of the afternoon two other people stood up to speak about what the treatment had done for them and how grateful they were, but by then I was numb and couldn't cope with much more emotion.

I spent the next four hours going round the room and talking to everyone and being hugged to death. The trouble makers had indeed turned up and I had spotted them immediately they arrived but I think they must have realised that if they had said anything publicly they would have been jumped on by everyone there. Colm, Di, and Charlie were as good as their word and kept that group of people tied up in knots so they never had a chance to move from the table at which they had sat themselves. I didn't go anywhere near them and they didn't make any attempt to approach me throughout the afternoon. They were not people on my trial and hadn't been invited to the party but I knew who they were and how they had found out about the event. I was so busy with the people who were there to celebrate that I didn't give the trouble makers a second's thought. There were three people there who hadn't shown any improvement as a result of the treatment and I considered it immensely brave of them to come to the party. As the afternoon wore on they or their partners came to me and told me how wonderful it was for them to speak to people the treatment was working for and that it had given them hope again. The highlight of the afternoon was when a girl, Linda, who had come all the way from Scotland, came up to me and asked if I would make an announcement over the public address system. I said that of course I would and asked her what she wanted me to say. She giggled and told me that she wanted me to challenge her friend, Graham, who was with her to do a cartwheel! Apparently he had been saying that he had recovered so well on my treatment that he should be able to do cartwheels. I went up to the microphone and said, "I have been asked to issue a challenge to Graham to come up and do a cartwheel for us." I fully expected Graham to refuse and was amazed when he jumped up and took off his jacket. He walked into the middle of the hall and promptly did a cartwheel across the floor! The place erupted with people yelling, cheering and whistling at him. I was so caught up in the moment that I went up to the mike and said, "That was amazing, Graham, but we all know that if something good happens, neurologists will simply say it was a fluke. So could you please do it again to provide the proof?" Once again people started clapping and cheering as Graham got to his feet again and executed another perfect cartwheel. I very much doubt if you could go to any other meeting of people with MS and witness an event like that again.

It was a couple of days later when Gill and I were talking about the party and how those people must have felt that she said, "We came, we saw and we realised it had been conquered". I guess she was right. There was no way that anyone at the party could deny the reality of what the treatment had done for so many people.

I felt extremely uncomfortable about being awarded celebrity status. As far as I was concerned I had been astonishingly lucky in tripping over the particular combination of drugs and being able to work out what was going on but I saw it as no more than that. I also felt the immense responsibility that went with what I had discovered. I was overwhelmed by the sheer numbers of people who were contacting me and expecting me to have the answer to their prayers. There were times when I wanted to scream at them "Leave me alone! I'm only human and there is one of me but tens of thousands of you" and there were even times when I seriously wished I had never discovered the treatment.

The day after the party was the biggest anti-climax of my life. I didn't know how to get back to normal life after the party and everything that had gone with it. I felt in limbo and almost depressed. I knew that I had to do something boring and mundane to get back in touch with reality so I went for a walk down Oxford Street. As it was a Sunday not many shops were open so I went into Virgin Megastore to look at CDs. I felt that I could legitimately spend some money on a couple of CDs as I was incapable of working without music playing in the background and I had to get on with writing this book. I had played my current music to death and needed to find a new theme song to work to. I had some songs that I always fell back on like Queen, "Don't Stop Me Now", T'Pau, "China in Your Hands", Paul Simon "The Obvious Child," and Pink Floyd, "Shine on You Crazy Diamond". I would put the CD on and play the track on continous repeat until I was sick of it, which normally meant several hours later. I emerged from the shop clutching several CDs which promptly became my new work music. This whole book was written over the space of four weeks while listening to "Never Forget" the new single by Take That, and "Love is All Around" by Wet Wet Wet! I had been playing the Take That single for some days before I truly began to hear the words and they struck me as astoundingly appropriate to my situation. The chorus in particular became my theme. It talks about never forgetting where you have come from and not falling into the trap of believing that what you are experiencing now is real. The chorus ends by saying that someday soon this will all be someone else's dream, we're not invincible, we're only people. I guess that summed up for me where I was at.

It was three weeks after the party that I received a letter from Fiona who had travelled all the way from Scotland to be there. She had sent me a copy of an article she had written for a local MS Newsletter. She wrote:

"At 7 am on Saturday, 2 September, I boarded an airplane at Dalcross airport on a voyage of discovery. Those of you who know me will be aware that during the past year I have suffered a severe relapse, resulting in two spells of hospitalisation, months of physiotherapy and, against my better judgement, a short course of steroids—all to no avail. This necessitated the eventual use of a wheelchair. I have always, however, had the absolute belief that I would someday, somehow get better."

Fiona had then written about how she heard about me and how she came to be on my trial. She continued,

"Having now been on the treatment for three and a half months I can tell you honestly that I have improved significantly and am continuing to do so. On meeting Cari now you would never know there had ever been anything wrong with her. She was literally dancing around and is such a vivacious character she is

inspirational. The whole day was full of wonderful stories and optimism. I can say to you all, be patient, the future looks bright. I believe there is a light at the end of the tunnel at last."

I thought what she had written was wonderfully full of optimism and hope for the people who have yet to get hold of the treatment. Fiona had written on the bottom of the typed letter,

"Am about to do away with the wheelchair! I am amazing the physiotherapist and myself with my almost daily improvement. I think you can even read my writing again now!. Here's to the healing power of lateral thinking."

◆

EPILOGUE

◆

L OOKING BACK back to October 1992 when I first woke
up with what I later found out was MS seems like a
thousand years ago and yet it is, in reality, less than three
years. As for thinking about the twenty-two months with MS it
all seems like a bad dream now. In writing this book I have had
to relive everything and try and get back in touch with the way I
felt. It has horrified me at times how I have indeed been able to
re-experience those feelings of fear and sadness and rage. There
are things that I have written about, such as feeling suicidal, that
I didn't want to remember. On the other hand remembering
parts of the story has had me laughing out loud as I sat in front of
my computer typing this. Sometimes these days I lie in bed at
night with the lights out and try and remember what my life used
to be like. I know the kind of things that used to matter to me,
like deadlines at work, or landing a research contract, or wanting

to be a vice-chancellor, but I can no longer understand why they mattered so much.

I know that the experience of having MS has completely changed my priorities for the better. What matters to me these days is being able to do the little things in life, like running upstairs, or not wanting to fall asleep an hour after having woken up, or being able to pick up Alice, my two-year-old niece, to cuddle her without the fear of falling over or dropping her. I guess the old saying that you don't know what you've got 'til it's gone is true. I, like every other able bodied person, had taken my body's ability to function for granted before MS hit. When I was almost incapable of walking I would look out of the window in my flat and watch people racing along the road and would want to shout at them, "Don't take it for granted. Make the most of it and enjoy it. You never know when it might be taken away from you." I truly regretted the fact that while I had been fit and healthy I had coasted along and never really made the most of the physical abilities that I had. Nor had I been bothered about looking after my body properly. I had been overly concerned about the way I looked in terms of not being thin enough, but once the MS struck I didn't give a damn.

Paradoxically, having MS gave me much greater self-confidence than I had ever previously known. I had always known I was a fighter but what I was able to do during my time with MS amazed me. I have always said that if anyone had asked me before I got MS if I would be able to cope with it, I would have said that there was no way I could handle anything like that. Well, I *did* cope with it quite well on the whole. People would tell me how brave I was and I had to point out to them that it was nothing to do with being brave. When you are faced with something like MS there are only ever three choices, get on with it as best you can, give up and vegetate, or kill yourself. I have encountered a few people who have MS who have allowed it to make them incredibly bitter. The bitterness is the one thing we can surely do something about, that we can refuse to give in to. Sometimes I look at children who have been born with physical handicaps and observe the way they cheerfully fight on and wonder why we as adults seem to be incapable of doing that?

And sometimes I wish I had a crystal ball so I could see what the situation will be in three years' time after the clinical trials have been completed and, all being well, the treatment is available to everyone who needs it. I find it impossible to believe that the trials will fail, as the outcome of my independent trial to date has been so astonishing. My greatest dream is that in due course MS will be treated like any other manageable disease and a diagnosis of it will not mean that your life will be destroyed to a greater or lesser degree. Maybe then slogans like the MS Society one implying that MS is a living hell will not be necessary. I am not claiming to have found a cure for MS, or even the ultimate treatment for it, but until something better comes along my treatment seems to be a pretty good stop gap solution. I think that all of us with MS can say, with our hands on our hearts, that so long as we can get enough of our former ability back to be able to function independently at a reasonable level and for a reasonable period of time, we will be happy. I also firmly believe that when doctors know that there is a treatment available that can prevent the relentless slide to disablement, they will be much more willing to diagnose MS earlier and actually tell the patient what they have got. That surely has to be a bonus for both them and their patients.

As I have been writing this book, it has made me focus very clearly on what has happened to me over the past three years. It has been a bizarre experience as I have been forced to analyse things from a distance. The thing that astonishes me the most is that I firmly believe that if the MS came back now for some reason I would cope with it no better than I did the first time round. Maybe I am wrong but I do not think I am strong enough to cope with being put through all that again. I have immense respect and admiration for the people I have met who have been dealing with MS for decades and are still coping and getting on with their lives. I hope I have learned some lessons from them that will allow me to be stronger when facing other apparently impossible situations in my life. I do know that I will never forget the power of being able to see the ludicrous side of situations. I also know that I have much less sympathy for people who whinge and whine about trivial complaints. Maybe that is not a good thing but frankly I can't be bothered with people who make a song and dance about the fact that they have a sprained or even broken ankle, or a migraine or even something more serious but that can be treated and from which they will recover. They don't know how lucky they are. In a perverse way I wish that everyone in the world had to go through what I went through for twenty-two months. I think the world would be a much nicer place and people would be far more tolerant of each other. Certainly I am almost evangelical now about things like public access and equal opportunites for people with disabilities. People with disabilities are not something to be scared of. If you meet a person who has trouble speaking clearly then I beg you not to be embarrassed but to take the time to listen and talk to them like you would to any other human being. If you see someone staggering or falling on the street don't assume they are drunk and turn away. Try putting yourself in the position of that person for a moment. How would you want to be treated? Is it fair to expose someone to prejudice and ridicule who is already trying to cope with an illness that they had no choice about getting? Don't think that you are invincible, tomorrow you may be struck by a disease of the nervous system or hit by a car when crossing the road and end up paraplegic. Let's face it, even Superman ended up paralysed. I suppose one of the biggest lessons that has been brought home to me is that you can never know what is around the next corner and to a large extent there is nothing you can do to change the way it is going to be. Once I was hit by MS I bitterly regretted some of the opportunities that I had turned down in my life. I had never participated in sports and yet, once I could barely walk, more than anything I wanted to be able to run. We all seem to live believing that we can put things off until tomorrow or until we have more time. The problem is that we can never be sure that there will be a tomorrow. If you take the opportunity today and your life is destroyed tomorrow, at least you will have the memories. I have met people who are in wheelchairs as they are unable to walk, who tell me that they can still walk in their dreams. The memories are still there.

When I consider my future these days I find it impossible to guess what it is going to be like. People are talking to me about appearing on television, being interviewed on the radio and conducting book signings. I look at my possible financial future, if the trials go according to plan and the treatment appears on the market, and I normally crack up laughing. I really don't believe that any of these things will actually happen. But, on the other hand, I can't deny that in just over a month's time I will be giving up half my job at the Institute of Education. I reckon that getting my life back from MS is all I could ever want and that anything else is simply the icing on the cake. I don't care about the money that might come my way. What can money really buy for you? It certainly couldn't give me my body back when MS destroyed it. Material posessions mean nothing to me these days. There was a time when I would have gladly given up everything I owned just to be able to walk normally again and, if faced with the same choice again, I know that I would feel the same.

I still go through times when I can't believe that my treatment works for other people. I know I have the evidence as I have met the people whose lives it has changed, but I find it impossible to believe that this is something that I have done. Can the answer to such a complex disease really be this easy at the end of the day? It almost doesn't seem right that the solution was this simple – although I reiterate that the treatment is not a cure. All I can say is that for the past thirteen months I have been able to live with no disability and no further attacks and, as far as I am concerned, I don't have to know that I have MS. How can there be anything wrong with me when I can run, jump, dance and work like a maniac without any problems at all? How can I still have an incurable, paralysing disease when I am physically no different from any other healthy person? To be honest, I feel better now than I have for my entire life before MS. Even my consultant neurologist can't find any physical signs left that I have MS. When people who hear about my story ask me these days if I have MS I have to do a double take and tell them that yes I do. Part of me wants to tell them that I *used* to have MS because that is the way I think of it!

I now believe that there was a purpose in my having MS. I had to get it. My life had to be the way it was. I truly believe that I have been used by some power out there. Call it God or Buddha or Allah or whatever you want; I call it the Northern Lights. For whatever reason it seems to have decided to give those of us with

MS a break at long last. I know that everyone on my treatment who is recovering is saying their own private thank you, to whatever power they can relate to, in whatever way is appropriate for them. They know that it wasn't me that did this, although they are grateful to me for battling on with it and telling them about it. All I can say is that I feel immensely privileged to have been used to do this, privileged, humbled and completely overwhelmed. I know the future is safe because the Northern Lights are still shining on us. But I have learned a valuable personal lesson about the nature of this power. It won't snap its fingers and make things better but, if you work with it and keep your part of the bargain, it will help to make things happen. I know that when I sat back for a while and waited for my Northern Lights to deliver the next amazing event, everything ground to a halt. My part of the bargain was to keep working very hard and keep driving things forward. It wasn't going to make things easy for me. In fact it expected a hell of a lot from me. There were times when I was in tears through the pressure and exhaustion and would plead with it to remember that I was only human and that there was a limit to what I could do. The message would come back that I wasn't on my own, that this was a partnership and then, out of the blue, another person would come into my life who would give me the support I needed.

I sometimes think about the advisers I have working with me and can't believe that I know so many wonderful people now. John, my patent agent; David, my financial adviser; Nigel, my accountant; Jane, my literary agent; Malcolm, my producer; Mark, my editor, and David from Scotia. Every single one of them has contributed something unique to the process of developing the treatment. Not only have they given me exceptional professional service but they have supported me as friends. They have dealt patiently with my low moments as well as my highs. Most of all they have believed in me when I was losing confidence. And then there are the people on my trial. Many of them have become good friends who are as concerned about me as I am about them. I consider myself one of the luckiest people in the world.

Now that everything is in place to move forward with the treatment, it is easy to look back on the MS years and claim that none of it was that bad. That is what happens when, as Denni said, you can not only see the light at the end of the tunnel but have come out of it and are standing in the sunshine. I can honestly say now that I wouldn't have missed the experience of MS for anything. I don't deny that those twenty-two months with MS were a high price to pay, as I could only believe in the midst of it that the rest of my life had been taken away from me, but the outcome is that I may well have discovered the first effective treatment for MS in the history of the disease since its naming in 1827. I have said, from time to time, recently that if I were to find myself lying in hospital tomorrow with only hours left to live I would be happy as I could die knowing that my life had been worthwhile and I would have no regrets. I reckon that is the ultimate privilege in life.

Well, here I am at the end of the book. The end of a chapter in my life and, no doubt, the beginning of another, the title of which I can't even guess at yet. I regard my life these days with a mixture of amazement, wonderment and trepidation. Whatever happens from now on I know that I have done my best so far and hope that I am equal to the challenges that will face me during the coming years. I continue to talk to the Northern Lights about all the other people in the world who have MS, asking that they too can benefit the way I have. My Northern Lights shine on, reassuring me that all will be well. My intention is that one day I will go and see them and stand there to deliver a face to face thank you.

I'd like to thank you for reading my story. I wanted to write this book so that those of you with MS who have to wait a couple more years to get the treatment know that the finishing line is now in sight. Keep the faith, my friends. One day soon I hope that you will be able to say that you too are *standing in the sunshine*.